Praise for *Organizing the Good Life*

"Celia puts family at the top of the 'Good Life' list. Nurturing those you love is an excellent way to find joyful simplicity and Celia really shows you how in this impactful new book."

—Raymond Aaron, co-author,
Chicken Soup for the Parent's Soul

"Being a parent is forever, but the time your kids live at home with you goes by in a flash. Celia's book shares lots of creative ways to really be there for them during those precious, fleeting years. I loved reading about her fun, spontaneous approach to teaching—and learning from—her own little ones … she's as brilliant a mom as she is a writer!"

—Michele Borba, author,
Parents Do Make a Difference and
Building Moral Intelligence

"I opened it up to have a quick glance and couldn't put it down. The most genuinely helpful book I've ever seen. Left me full of resolutions and the wisdom to make them happen in my own life."

—Alex Hiam, author,
The Manager's Pocket Guide to Creativity

"I encourage you to read this book for the wisdom it contains. Celia Rocks provides the necessary steps needed to adopt a complete lifestyle transformation—while answering those tough questions we've all struggled with for improving the quality of our lives and finding true happiness, peace, and joy."

—Sue Fox, author,
Business Etiquette For Dummies

"It's so easy to get bored with the same ol' concepts. How many ways can we learn how to cut back and slow down? Well, Celia Rocks has found a better way. She has learned that getting b_ck _o _he b___cs i_ _o_r _u_ines_ and life doesn't mean having less stuff, it _ean_ _avin_ _mor_ of wh_t _eal_ matters."

—Jennifer White, author,
Work Less Make More

P
A
T
H
W
A
Y
S
to SELF-SUFFICIENCY

Funded by:
County of Huron
Pathways to Self-Sufficiency
program

W9-CPP-087

–» –» –» –» ⚜ «– «– «– «–

Dost thou love life? Then do not squander time,
for that's the stuff life is made of.
- *Benjamin Franklin, 1706-1790*

–» –» –» –» ⚜ «– «– «– «–

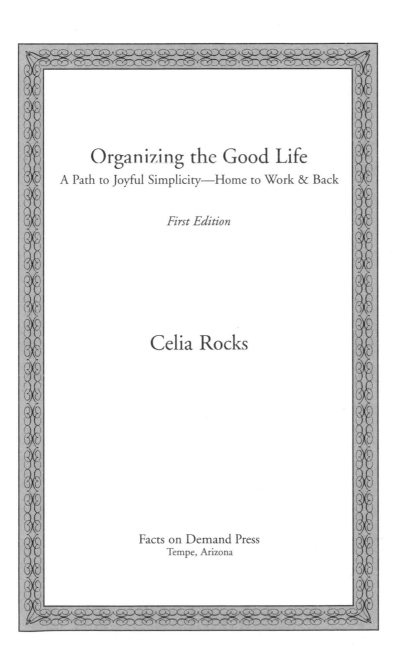

Organizing the Good Life

A Path to Joyful Simplicity—Home to Work & Back

First Edition

Celia Rocks

Facts on Demand Press
Tempe, Arizona

©2001 Celia Rocks

Facts on Demand Press
1971 E 5th Street, Suite 101
Tempe, AZ 85281
(800) 929-3811

ISBN 1-889150-26-6

Cataloging-in-Publication Data
Rocks, Celia
Organizing the good life: a path to joyful
simplicity—home to work & back / Celia Rocks.—1st ed. p. cm.

1-889150-26-6

1. Simplicity.   2. Conduct of life.   I. Title.

BJ1496.R63 2001   179'.9
                    QBI01-700466
Book Design: Andra Keller
Line Drawings: Jan Dickinson
Editorial Coordination: John Patrick Grace,
Grace Associates, Ltd., 945 4th Avenue, Suite 200A
Huntington, WV 25701 • (800) 394-6909

Foreword by
Carol Adrienne

You will get your money's worth, and more, from this book if you read only Chapter Two, "Show Up." This is where you put your foot on the path that leads to "a life that works"—a life of "joyful simplicity." It is also the chapter upon which the rest of the book is built—being ethical, deciding what's important, energizing your environment, knowing how to delegate, managing money, and getting your relationships right.

Showing up in life is the reminder that the energy we put out comes back to us a thousand-fold. I love actress Lily Tomlin's remark, "I always wanted to be somebody, but I should have been more specific."

Showing up is the key element that tells us when we are in alignment. When we are fully and authentically present, we bring together our experience, talents, desires, and internal resources to deal with whatever is happening—and we feel connected to what matters most to us. Not only that, but showing up means we are radiating out a certain vibration that will attract into our lives what we need for the next step. We are going to meet the people we need to meet. We are going to attract the opportunities that open us to the next level of life. Perhaps even more importantly, we're going to feel like we are following the purpose of our life.

Showing up is the first part of integrity and essential to commitment—both virtues that are intrinsically satisfying. When we search for meaning and we yearn to know what our purpose is, we'll never find it if we don't look within and find exactly what we need to be doing today—where we need to show up today. Showing up is both paying attention and setting an intention to live a great life every day—no matter whether it is during our walking, driving, gardening, teaching, parenting, researching, or bill-paying. Showing up in the present automatically helps us create the future, and usually heals the past, if we are truly living a balanced life. Just think for one moment about how fully present you have been in each encounter you've already had so far today. Were you deleting e-mails while you were having a phone conversation? Were you paying bills while you talked to your child after school? Are you procrastinating on a project, or are you really giving it "germination" time? Your internal integrity center knows exactly what the answer is!

The ability to show up depends on whether you are listening or not and what actions you are taking about what you hear. I know, for myself, I can hear the level of commitment when I tell a friend, "I'll try to call you later this week." Not very strong!

Celia and I worked together a few years ago on a media campaign for my book, *The Purpose of Your Life*. Working with someone is an excellent way to get to know something about his or her experience, skills, priorities, values, sense of humor, and dedication—and Celia passed my test in the first few conversations. This book is an outgrowth of her business and life experiences—not just with work and how to be productive and full of integrity. It also speaks on many levels about what it takes to be a person—and how to show up in our diverse roles, whether it be as a parent, business person, or friend. Her stories and suggestions ring true. The book emphasizes the importance of knowing what balance means to us—individually.

No one can live our lives for us, but we all need to have that little chat with a friend once in a while over a cup of tea. Celia helps us iron out some of those questions we would ask our best friend or our grandmother, if she weren't working out at the gym or traveling to Borneo!

Before you start to read this book, I'd suggest that you jot down one or two questions that are on your mind today (such as, How can I find more balance in my life?). Then write down three or four, or more, words about how you'd like to feel. Then go ahead and read the book. Your current life questions, desires, and goals will help to focus your subconscious as you read. You'll be even more likely to tune into how the stories and principles apply to yourself.

This book gives you a wide range of support in freeing yourself from the emotional drains of overwhelm, resentment, envy, guilt, work addiction, or the nagging self-doubt that tend to occur when you forget that it's in your hands to create the life you want.

Carol Adrienne is the co-author with James Redfield of the two main nonfiction companions to his enormously successful Celestine books. She conducts her popular seminar, "Uncover the Purpose of Your Life—How to Move Forward and Make the Changes You Want to Make." She is also an intuitive teacher and popular lecturer on spiritual matters and numerology. She lives in El Cerrito, California.

Works by Carol Adrienne:
The Purpose of Your Life
The Numerology Kit

Co-Authored with James Redfield
The Celestine Prophecy: An Experiential Guide

Dedication

This book is dedicated to my sister-in-law, Veronica Rocks, who, upon learning that she had cancer, immediately shut down her law office. "I don't want to spend one more day doing what I am not happy doing," she said. May she inspire you, as she has inspired me, to ask yourself these questions: "Why am I doing what I'm doing? Am I really happy with my life the way it is? And if not, how can I change it to make it right?"

Acknowledgements

I would like to thank my husband, Richard, for teaching me the relationship between organization and ultimate happiness. I would also like to thank my children, Frank and Elizabeth, for being so patient and understanding as I worked on this book.

And thank you, my dear clients, who gave me incredible insight into your individual areas of expertise. I could not have written this book without you.

Thanks to Dottie DeHart and Megan Johnson, who have mastered a balance of work and life that makes them a pleasure to work with every day.

Finally, thanks to Patrick Grace who "showed up" in my office one spring day and convinced me to write this book. He is a visionary editor. I couldn't and wouldn't have done it without him.

Contents

Preface

I love teaching people about creativity. You know, having dreams and figuring out how to make them happen. Dreams are nice enough on their own. But if you can get them to happen ... ah, that's so fulfilling and happy-making.

Today both couples and singles are struggling with creating a satisfying life. I see it all around me. Some people pick up one piece, others another piece. Like, a woman may learn to treat herself to massage therapy. A man may be real regular about jogging in the park. Or whatever. Still, a lot of Good Life components seem to escape them.

What I want to get across in this book is that *it is possible* to build yourself the life you dream about—where quality family time, wonderful outings, fulfilling work, and a healthy family balance sheet all come together. Believe me, if I could reform my life from the chaos it was eight years ago in Miami, so can you.

Achieving joyful simplicity is possible, however, no matter what the size of your city or town may be. As the saying has it, *Wherever you go, there you are.*

Few of you are as messed up as I was financially. Or as sold out to a junky materialistic style of life. Or as addicted to television watching. If I have created a satisfying Good Life, with my husband and children, balancing our society's witches' brew of work and home and social life, and making it fun, so can you. This book will take you through the steps that have worked for me.

You will see, as I finally did, that though you may never be counted among the truly rich, you can have all the benefits of a wealthy person *if you know how to prioritize what is important to you and structure your lifestyle around those values.* Remember, the only true reason to have money is for the emotional comfort it can bring you. So learn to make and use it wisely. You, like the very rich, can have "butlers" to whom you can delegate many everyday tasks. That will leave you time to use your talents to generate money. And time to nurture a spouse, children, or friends, and receive their love.

Make a pledge to yourself right now that you are going to do more than just buy this book. More than just read this book. *You are going to reform whatever is getting in the way of creating for yourself and your cherished ones a life that works.* You can do it, honey. I know you can.

Pittsburgh, Pennsylvania
June 2001

Organizing the Good Life
A Path to Joyful Simplicity—Home to Work & Back

CHAPTER ONE

Celia's Rise from Spendaholic to Doyenne of the Good Life

In the doldrums of my disorganized days, I kept a very large personal checkbook that was like a hardbound book. I actually carried it around with me. The reason I had this checkbook was that my lack of order was so bad that I would have lost a checkbook any smaller. Believe me, I tried using small checkbooks then. They would end up *under* the seat of my car. I'd find them when I dropped my car keys on the floor. And who knew where my car keys were half the time?

The large checkbook was a desperate step to figure out systems that worked for me and helped me to organize. I knew that I was on the road to a big reform program. I knew I was willing to work hard to have the things I wanted in life, but I knew that also meant I couldn't have it all. My mission was not to be *Superwoman* but rather to be the best I could be. I hope my steps in this book help you do the same.

I grew up on the streets of Miami. I didn't have a very disciplined home life. So my sense of boundaries was fuzzy. I went out a lot. I went everywhere. By age eight I was taking buses to the mall. By myself. In other words, I was a streetwise girl. By age sixteen I was starting college. And since that age I have basically taken care of myself, thank God. Put me on a street corner in London with a bit of cash in my pocket and I'll be just fine. Within a couple weeks I'll have a job and a nice flat. A lot of children who have grown up more or less on their own have this same gift of self-reliance.

After college and a variety of jobs and small-business experiences, I found myself working for Burson-Marsteller in Miami, the largest public relations agency in the world. I was driving a late-model Toyota and living in an apartment off the beach. It may seem to you like quite a life. Along the way, however, I was also racking up $35,000-plus in debt. It just happened. It seemed like "the normal thing," to be that much over my head in debt.

I would say to myself, "Well, this is just the way it is. This is the way people live nowadays. They see something, they buy it, they throw it onto the credit card. No big deal."

But it is a big deal. Thirty-five thousand dollars of debt becomes something like $70,000 when you add on the interest as you pay it off over eight or nine years.

I met my husband, Richard, in Miami. He was older than me, and had been married before. His way of life was different from mine. He spent his money in much more deliberate ways.

Richard might pay quite a lot for an item of clothing for himself or for a gift for someone else, but everything he bought was first class. High quality. He'd have only four pair of dress slacks at a time, no more. But they were very finely made. That's all he needed, four. I began to see that quality things would last—for a long, *long* time. Junk would not.

Richard's ways cast doubt on my penchant for buying whatever trinket might catch my eye. There had to be a better way.

I recognized that much of my debt had to do with buying things that were not worth much over time. With more careful purchasing, I could have better clothes and other possessions that would wear well for many years. And I saw that, ironically, buying the best might be a way to trim my debt.

By and by Richard and I had our son, Frank. When he was very small, living in Miami wasn't a problem. As he grew into a toddler who wanted to be outside playing a lot, I became warier of having him on the streets—even though the streets had been my own domain growing up. The crime rate in Miami was through the roof. I wanted to raise my son, and future offspring, in a safer atmosphere. Was that such a crazy idea?

Simultaneously, doctors told me that Miami sun was devastating my skin. What a shock! Here I was, a girl who'd lolled for hours on the wide sandy beaches of my childhood home, never dreaming I could live away from the ocean. I had such an affinity with the ocean; it was my *soul*. I had spent years working on a lobster fishing boat, being a tennis instructor, a scuba diver, a lifeguard. And then I developed this incurable allergy to infrared rays. Now these doctors were telling me I'd better stay out of the sun!

Richard and I started talking about finding another place to live.

The idea was that I would resign from Burson-Marsteller, and since Richard had his own heavy equipment sales company and was free to locate basically wherever he wanted, we would look for a livable small city that was a great place to raise kids. Then I would start my own public relations agency and we would go on from there. After a considerable search, we settled on Hickory, North Carolina. Hickory sits in the foothills of the Appalachian Mountain range midway between Winston-Salem and Asheville, and just a bit over an hour north of Charlotte. It's the home of Lenoir-Rhyne College, peaceful and simple. Air service out of Charlotte and Greensboro (just east of Winston-Salem) is good. A nice fit, and a great place for me to put into practice my hopes of creating a simpler, and more joyous, lifestyle. I had a hunch even then that some day I would be back in a big city, but I told myself, "This'll be great for now. I can see how this whole simplicity thing works, and then I'll be able to use it anywhere."

Most of what I offer in this book I learned from trial and error during these years in Hickory. Circumstances changed and my family and I changed with them, and now we are settled happily back in a big city, Pittsburgh. Richard grew up here and wanted to be near his family again. But I'm getting ahead of my story.

We moved to Hickory and rented a townhouse to give ourselves a chance to get the feel of the neighborhoods before we made a decision on buying a house. It was while we were living in this townhouse that our daughter, Elizabeth, was born. After a couple of years we purchased a modest but comfortable 2,000-square-foot home in a neighborhood of rolling hills and lots of great shady trees. It was perfectly ample; there was a nice living room, a full-sized kitchen with an eat-in area, a family room downstairs, a screened-in porch, a deck, and a big yard for the kids to play in. I mean, what else do you need? I rented office space a mere two miles from our house, and launched my agency.

Shortly after we moved in, I had a local fellow come over to clean our gutters. When he was done, I asked him, "How much?" I had trouble understanding his answer. Having come from living in Miami I was prepared for something like, "A hundred dollars." But what was he *saying? Twelve dollars!?!* I couldn't believe it.

That was one occasion when I recognized that I had been living with an attitude that constant spending was the way you achieved happiness. But in the joyful world inhabited by people who had a perspective of simplicity, you just did not need to throw money around the way quite a few did in south Florida.

"What an amazing combination!" I said to myself. What if I could take my earning potential, continue to earn it, but change the way I spent money. Are you with me now? Are you getting this? I realized a simple truth: *I could have a really satisfying life if I just called a halt to my high consumer ways.*

Another day early in our settling in at Hickory, I spotted a man sitting by the side of the road selling firewood out of his pickup truck. For $70, he would sell you the whole load, and even deliver it to your house. I kept thinking, "How much income does this man make if he has to chop down a tree, cut it up, sit by the roadside to sell it, and then actually deliver the wood to somebody's house?" I figured that the man had the luxury of working with his hands precisely because he did not have the credit card debt that I did. I guarantee you he didn't.

At the same time, though, contrary to my new insights on consumerism, I was continuing to carry home more "stuff" each week, things I had bought at the mall. After marking a little time in our house, many of these trinkets would gravitate up to our attic. Richard would go up there periodically, and, I thought, sort through things. But his approach was far more drastic. One day he said to me, "Listen, you know all that stuff that was in the attic? I threw it all out. I gave it to Goodwill today."

"You did WHAT!?!" I screamed.

"Well, what did you have up there?"

Do you know, most of it, I couldn't even remember. I didn't know what I had in storage.

So Richard said, "Well, if you need any of those things again, I'll go out and buy them for you. I'll replace for you whatever I tossed; just tell me what you want."

Somehow, I never asked him to go out and buy me another copy of a trinket or cheap sweater that he had tossed.

Along with watching my husband remake my buying habits, I also set myself a serious goal: I would get out of debt. All the way. As it turned out, accomplishing this goal was to take me six years. That may seem like a long time, but unless you start your debt-reduction program today, I can promise you that six years from now you'll be no better off than you are right now—and your debt may even be worse.

"So what about your new P.R. agency?" you ask. Well, I found myself in the furniture-making area of North Carolina, so I expected that what I would do would be to publicize good furniture. Broyhill, for example, is a local manufacturer. Broyhill came out with a new line and wanted to get the word all around. Advertising is expensive. P.R., I assured the company, was a better way to go. Broyhill is now our client of eight years along with many other name-brand companies.

With P.R., though, often you have to travel. Let's say a franchise is opening a new store in Tennessee, and they hire you to promote the event. You have to go to the site and be on hand to support the efforts. It takes you away from home. As a mother, my top priority was figuring out how to spend more time with my children, not less. There's one product that is different, however: books. If you are promoting books, you, the P.R. person, don't have to go to any site. They don't want you. They want the author—and the book. Actually, I never even thought about promoting books as part of my public-relations venture.

However, shortly after I moved to Hickory, an old client of mine, Eric Rhoads in Florida, sent me a copy of a book he had just published on the 75th Anniversary of Radio. The book was a pictorial history of radio in America.

"Celia," he said, "I need somebody to publicize this book. Can you help?" So I said, "Well, why not?"

I was able to get articles and reviews about Eric's book into magazines and newspapers all over the country. During this time, Eric was attending a book seminar and managed to bring up my work with John Kremer, who wrote the book, *1,001 Ways to Market Your Book.* And my networking began.

He also referred me to the people who were putting out the ... *For Dummies* line of books. They hired me to promote their popular line of yellow & black books. A one-book project turned into twenty books, and just like that, my firm was representing one of the fastest-growing publishers in North America.

Once you have a contract with a large, creative, innovative, and rapidly expanding publisher, everybody else wants to join in. Success breeds success. (However, be realistic: You're not going to wake up one morning and be a "success" without working as hard and as smart as you can every day.)

And Rocks-DeHart Public Relations' specialty in business and lifestyle book promotion took off from there. Now, it's most of what we do. Over time I've built up the staff to four full-time people and five part-timers, all very creative, all hard working, which is what you need in a P.R. firm.

The me that just "had to live by the ocean" was gone. The me that was stuck in gargantuan, suffocating debt was on her way out. However, the workaholic Celia was still hanging in there, fighting against the tide of sanity that was sweeping into my consciousness.

I was the type that hardly took a moment to breathe. I'd be at the office, morning, noon, and into the evening when I thought my workload called for it. Often (in *my* mind) it did. It was a really terrible time of my life. Here I was, being recognized as a leader in my industry, with the phone ringing off the hook, naming my own price. But I was totally out of synch with what was good for me. So one day I was on the phone with a client, Carol Adrienne, who had written the book, *The Purpose of Your Life.*

"You know," I told her. "I'm working sooo hard. I'm feeding off the frenzy."

Do you know what she said? She said, "Celia, why don't you just go home?"

"What?!?"

"Go home, Celia. The world will go on. Take the day off."

I have a lot of respect for Carol and her counseling work and what she had written in her book, so I took her advice. It went straight against the grain of my inbred workaholism, but I locked up the office and drove home in the middle of the morning.

I made myself a cup of coffee and turned on the TV. On *C-Span* there was a book show. They were doing a panel discussion, a program which, I later found out, had been taped several months earlier. And there, on the screen, was my client, Carol Adrienne.

Amazingly, the panel was talking about finding book publicists. One woman said, "You need to find a publicist who is good for you, who understands you."

And Carol starts talking about how, yes, she agrees, and how she has found one, "a great one who lives in Hickory, North Carolina."

Talk about serendipity!

That was the moment when I realized that you have to stop fighting what's good for you, like taking time off, like relaxing with a cup of coffee in the middle of the day. You have to pick up on the flow in your life, and go with it. Why are we all in such a hurry? What are we all killing ourselves for? What good is more money if you collapse of a heart attack or a stroke in your fifties ... or if your children don't want to spend time with you when they grow up?

-» -» -» -» ❦ «- «- «- «-

The joyful simplicity approach does not mean that six months after you finish reading this book, you'll have $50,000 in the bank, an IRA, and your whole household in apple-pie shape, and everything will be hunky-dory. Remember, when I started, I didn't own a home yet, though I was already thirty-four years old, and I was about $35,000 in consumer debt.

Important lifestyle change takes time.

If you try to rush it, and get everything patched up all at once, all you will do is generate massive frustration. Believe me. In this book, though, we'll go through the steps to creating more abundance for you, all the while simplifying the systems you use to run your life. Begin doing one small thing at a time. The process builds. Stay with it. It might take you several years—even five or six. But you'll get there, and you'll be glad you made the trip!

From here on we will continue the book using a literary device that goes back in time but was especially popular in the sixteenth and seventeenth centuries: a small cast of characters engaging in dialogue, with one being a teacher figure and the others playing the role of students (except these students sometimes challenge, even disagree with, the teacher!). I'll be the teacher figure in these hypothetical conversations (although sometimes when you think you're teaching, you're actually learning). For the other characters I'm going to use the names of people I know. These conversations are ficticious and were created to help you learn techniques that have helped me.

CHAPTER TWO

Show Up: It Is 80 Percent of Everything

Roy, my lawn-care man when I lived in Hickory, was sweeping my driveway on a superb September afternoon, and, with a cold drink in hand, I was standing by chatting as he worked. I love talking to Roy. He is so "real world." He loves working with the earth and growing things. Roy keeps it simple and peaceful.

"Like that cool breeze, Ma'am?" Roy said. "And look at those yellows and reds just startin' to come out on those trees." I could only agree. Autumn is a great time of year.

I especially like watching Roy work because he reminds me of two things that are very important for any activity. The first is doing whatever you're doing with all of your heart. The second follows naturally from that: paying careful attention and maintaining focus.

When Roy does something as simple as raking leaves, he really bears down on it. His rake moves in swift efficient strokes. Not even the tiniest stray leaf tucked into the grass escapes his

13

attention. When Roy prepares soil for planting, he treats it like gold dust.

So I like to tell myself, and I advise my colleagues, "When you say 'yes,' say it with all your heart. When you listen, listen with all your heart."

This is the essence of "showing up" for other people.

One day recently I was on the phone with a client and I was multi-tasking—checking my e-mail while I spoke with him about his book project. He interrupted the flow of our conversation to ask me, "What are you doing? You're not paying attention to me. What else are you doing besides speaking on the phone?"

When I confessed that I had been reviewing e-mails as we spoke, he said, "Listen, if you seriously want to listen from the heart, you need to do nothing else while you're on the phone but pay attention to that conversation." I have also had clients tell me it's even better if you can look at a picture of the person you're speaking to; I'm able to do this easily because most of my clients have their pictures on their books or websites. (Take a look at *my* website, www.CeliaRocks.com, and you'll see my picture right away.)

What are cell phones all about? Doing two things at once, right? Driving while talking on the phone. Trying to finish a meal at a restaurant while talking on the phone. Now don't get me wrong. I have a cell phone myself. There are times when there's no other phone handy and that's what I have to use. But apply the same principle: Show up for whoever's on the other end by paying attention and shutting down other activities. If you're in a car, park and talk from the curb. It's safer anyway. If you're in a restaurant, get away from other people—take your phone back by the pay phone and talk from there. If you're driving your children to school, treasure the moment by having a conversation with them. How many parents are constantly on the phone when their children are in the car? This is not a good example to set for impressionable young minds.

Here's another example of how to "show up" for children. When you're talking to children, stoop or bend so that you're on their level. Then look directly into their faces, instead of talking to them "from on high." You'll have much better rapport.

Recently I was invited to present my work as a book publicist at a seminar in New York. I bonded with a lot of people in the audience in the mixing time following my talk. The way I made sure that I was connecting well with people is that I paid attention to each person, one on one. I had—and expressed— a genuine interest in each individual. I asked each one a lot of questions about his or her background and current work. Just for "showing up" well at the event, I acquired important contacts with authors. These led to my first excursion as a literary agent and the subsequent closing of two major book contracts, with a 15 percent commission on each.

You can show up for your children by volunteering to help out in their classrooms. And the teachers will love you for it. You can show up for your community by volunteering to help with the March of Dimes neighborhood drive or pitch in on some other important effort—coaching Little League, joining the League of Women Voters, becoming a Big Brother or a Big Sister. There are lots of opportunities.

We've all heard the saying, "showing up is 80 percent of everything." I think we've got it wrong: showing up is *95 percent* of everything. Whatever percentage you put on it, it's extremely important.

There are definitely two kinds of people in this world: those who show up—and those who don't. Showing up takes energy. Sometimes, it takes a *lot* of energy. People who show up typically get up fairly early in the morning; they are into the shower early, and into their day. They have a lot they want to accomplish. O.K., all you night owls. I can hear you moaning. Nonetheless I firmly believe that following the natural cycle of the sun's light with your daily routine does have its place—and has been effective for thousands of years. (God's idea, not mine!)

When you "show up," you'll find that you meet the right people; you make yourself available for them to come into your life. You'll meet people who can help you grow, in your work and in the rest of your life. They'll help you focus on using your time and talents well. That in turn will (or at least *should*) result in your making valuable friendships and a rich contribution to the world.

In business especially, showing up is crucial. You need to be "at your business" as much as you can (even if your "business" is being a great employee). I see many people making the mistake of not being available to their clients, customers, or prospects. They're always out of reach—gone someplace or not available by phone or fax when others could reasonably expect them to be.

Myself, I check my e-mail frequently. Some people claim it breaks up their day to be checking e-mail. All I can tell you is in my particular business it works to check often. I have occasions when an e-mail is urgent. It may be a client asking if I can handle a certain piece ASAP, like, "Hey, can you get this done this afternoon?"

A client e-mailed me recently to see if I could handle a major project. I got right back to her and said, "Sure we can! We can start tomorrow!" And then I faxed her an agreement.

Because I was *there*, because I *showed up*, because I was able to say an enthusiastic, *"Yes, we'll get on it right now!"* my agency received a large volume of business. Then do you know what else happens? You become known for your rapid response. You earn a reputation for being not only available, but *eagerly* available. It makes a difference.

"Celia, hello. This is Allen. Have you got a minute?" Allen is one of our neighbors, a hardworking, but not always smart-working, nice guy.

"Sure, Allen," I said. "What's happening?"

"Listen, I'm about to incorporate my business, Celia. I was just about to spend some money on a local attorney when I saw an ad in a business paper. These people can incorporate you in any one of the fifty states, and they'll charge a lot less than a corporate attorney might. Can you believe that? I mean, is that a great deal or what? I thought I'd ask you to look at the ad and tell me what you think. I can bring it to your office or whatever, just let me know...."

"Allen, stay put. I don't need to see the ad. I can tell you what I think right from here."

"You can? Without even seeing the ad? Wow! That's some kind of intuition. I mean, don't you even want me to read you the text of the ad? It's pretty short."

"Allen, forget it. I've been there. I almost went that route myself—when I incorporated my agency. I was looking around town for a good attorney to incorporate us when I happened to be talking to a business associate of mine. He waved me off from my lawyer search. He said, 'All you need to do is call this company in Delaware. They'll do your incorporation very quickly via mail.'

"He went on and on about what a sweet deal this was. So I said to myself: Well, OK. He probably knows what he's talking about. I called the company and sure enough they shipped me all the materials for incorporation. And there I sat in my home with what seemed like five hundred pieces of paper about incorporating my business. A zoo!

"The next day I happened to stop by the office of a local attorney on a matter that had to do with the lease for my office. I mentioned to him that I was incorporating my business through this office in Delaware because it was very inexpensive. Do you know what that attorney said?"

"No, what?" Allen replied. "That he could match their price?"

I laughed. "No, Allen. He said, 'Don't you think this important process is worth paying an expert for?' And he was absolutely right. I threw all those forms in the trash, and that attorney incorporated our company. He took care of the lease and he took care of the incorporation. That relieved me of all the anguish of trying to get those forms filled out right. It also was a great comfort to know that I had secured a local attorney who knows the ropes and who became familiar with my business structure. As Dottie, my business partner, always says, 'Find and value expertise.'

"I'm not a tax person. I do public relations. Having an attorney handle our incorporation took a weight off my shoulders, and freed me up to do what I do best."

"I don't know, Celia. The Delaware deal still sounds pretty good to me."

"Delaware, schmelaware, Allen. That's not how I want to lead my life. Besides, let's take this scenario one step further. You let the local attorney incorporate you, handle your lease, be current on your tax situation and other business matters, and you stop in to see him from time to time. He comes to understand your business, the kind of life you're trying to have. It's a relationship.

"Now let's say that attorney is at a major social function one night. He talks to one business person after another. He mentions you and your work in conversations and that you are one of his clients. The money you paid him for work well done could easily translate into new business for your firm. Even if it doesn't become new business, though, knowing that his expertise has given you great value is enough. More importantly still, suppose you suddenly find yourself in need of immediate legal help. Well, you have a good lawyer who can plunge in and give you great advice."

Whether or not Allen was thoroughly convinced I'm not at all sure. What I'm more concerned about right now is that you are convinced. Believe me, doing your incorporation yourself at home on the dining room table is *not* "showing up."

"Showing up" is getting the word out there about what your own skills are, what *you* can handle. Meeting people and letting them know what you can do. And one of the best ways to do this is to let the right people into your life. Like that local attorney. He was very much one of the "right people," and has indeed been a great source of expertise for my agency.

"Mom, can we have a Hot Pocket®?" Out of the blue, Frank and Elizabeth had materialized from wherever they'd been playing around our house.

Being a mother is extremely important to me. Do you know what? We women who work outside the home are trying to do the impossible. It's next to impossible to be both a great manager or consultant, for example, and also be a great mom. Some of us achieve dancing on this high wire, but not without a lot of creativity and sacrifice.

"Sure," I told Frank and Elizabeth. "But just one each. Dinner's not far away." I was glad they asked for a Hot Pocket because the microwave is one of the few things I've actually mastered in the kitchen.

Richard, my husband, has to be away a lot to make his heavy equipment business succeed. When he is home, however, he is extra-attentive to our children. He has a thing, for instance, about tucking them each in at night and making them feel as secure as possible before going to bed. He puts a lot of attention into making sure that they are arranged in bed as comfortably as possible. That is one of the ways he expresses his love.

For me, this is really "showing up" for your children. Letting them know, in very specific, concrete ways that you care the world for them.

In similar ways spouses or people in a dating relationship can "show up" for each other. Attentive listening, thoughtful gift-giving, and tuning in to other's needs (for affection, time alone, recreation…) all constitute "showing up." Are you starting to get this picture?

I know people whose main preoccupation is always to "get away from the kids." They hire babysitters right and left and go out all the time. Life, you know, is long enough. I'll have plenty of time to be away from my children. I'm at a time in my life now when I need to be *near* my children as much as possible.

Can I tell you a story about my son, Frank? Richard and I were looking at other houses in our Hickory neighborhood. We thought maybe we would "trade up." Get ourselves a bigger house. Some people would say to me, "You really need to find a house where your bedroom doesn't share a wall with a child's room. That's a negative."

So I asked Frank, "Would you like us to get a bigger house?"

"No, Mom," he said. "I like being near you."

Then I thought, "How wonderful that we have a relatively small house, where I can be near my son at night and hear him talk to me from his bedroom!"

When I'm an old woman, I'll remember when my son was seven years old, and at night, when I was about to go to sleep, he would talk to me from his bedroom, and he could hear me say something back.

In our subsequent relocation to Pittsburgh, we did not experience any fear of being in too small a space—such as the apartment we took at the outset. Small is beautiful, as the title of a best-selling book had it.

Here's another way I learned to "show up" for my children. Richard and I decided when both our children were quite young that we would like to have them study the violin. Our home in Hickory was near Lenoir-Rhyne College, which has a school of music and also offers music lessons for children.

Because of my intense professional life, I thought it would be best to have my babysitter pick up my children from school, drive them over to Lenoir-Rhyne, and then sit through their violin lessons with them. Nonetheless, I was to be the one who would supervise their practices at home.

And then one day, it simply weighed in on me that taking Frank and Elizabeth to violin lessons was something that I should not delegate, but should do myself. So I blocked out time every Friday afternoon and left early from work so that I could accompany them to their lessons. It made a measurable difference in their performance, and I was then much better equipped to monitor their practices at our home.

My decision to be present for their violin lessons also led to the title for this book. While I was sitting in the practice room waiting for my children to start their lesson, I began to chat with the woman who was just packing up her little girl's violin from the previous lesson. I mentioned that I was working on a book, and told her some of the themes I would explore.

"Oh!" she said. "What you're doing is teaching people about 'organizing the good life.'"

The way she captured the essence of my message really resonated with me. And now her words are on the front cover of this book.

->> ->> ->> ->> ❧ <<- <<- <<- <<-

There is a flip side to the "showing up" equation. It is knowing when to say "no." No, I cannot meet you for lunch. No, you're not a client we can take on. No, I can't be at that meeting on May 25th because that's my daughter's graduation from kindergarten.

In other words, you must establish some sane boundaries, or you will go crazy. Especially if you are very good at what you do.

A man called not long ago from a city about an hour away from my office, after he had heard me being interviewed on the radio. "We're in the same kind of business!" he said. "Look, I live a little south of where you are. Can you drive down and have lunch?"

I made a mistake. I said, "Yes." At that point we had all the business we could handle, and I really did not have the three hours available to meet him for lunch (a one-hour drive each way, and one hour for our lunch meeting). After I'd told him I could do it, I looked at my calendar, and everything was full. Only then did it occur to me that what I *should* have said was, "Maybe we can talk on the phone," or, "I really can't get away; however, if *you* are free to drive up to my location, *then we can have lunch and talk in person.*"

Because I had committed to meeting him on his turf I honored the obligation, but I got home so late I missed hours of work and, subsequently, dinner with my family. You can bet that the next time a similar situation arose, I gave a firm and friendly "no."

Being a P.R. person, my instinct is usually to say, "Yes, we can do it." However, if you say "yes" to everybody, pretty soon you will have time for nobody.

It's a matter of boundaries. (And, remember, I did not grow up with a healthy sense of such.) Your day is a twenty-four-hour pie. Whatever you allocate to one part of your life (clients, prospecting, working with your accountant, or time with family, friends, and time to yourself) cannot be given away to another part of your life—without someone suffering the consequences.

I think it's important to give people some parameters about when you can be available to them. If you find yourself interrupting your reading of a bedtime story to your children to take a non-emergency phone call, you may want to rethink your boundaries, and set them to protect your family time. Even in the office, I've learned that if you give your business callers the boundaries of your availability, they will work within them. When you make calls, it's a good practice to ask, "Is this a good time for you to talk?" When I leave voice mail messages I always let people know good times to call back.

I've gotten better over the years. Now, if a client calls me and says she needs us to rush-rush on something and get it finished that afternoon, I may say, "I try to do my best to make things happen for you, but I have to keep track of my irreplaceable priorities. Today, for instance, there is a late afternoon basketball game I want to go to, because my son is playing."

Often, there is a middle way—a way of saying, "No, I can't be there," and yet still "showing up." I'll give you an example: One Monday I was supposed to go and pick up my son's baseball trophy from his coach's office, which was fairly far from my office. I had a jammed-up Monday and really was hard put to get away, so I delegated the trophy retrieval to my errand runner. The problem with that, of course, was that I couldn't thank the coach in person for all his great work with my son, Frank.

So I sat down and wrote the coach a note—on elegant personal stationery. I wrote, "I'm so sorry I wasn't able to pick up the trophy personally. I want to thank you for all your hard work this year helping my son at the catcher's position and also the way you helped all his teammates on the baseball team.

Best regards - Celia Rocks."

That note represented me as well as I could on that occasion. And it allowed me to "show up." Guideline: If you somehow cannot "show up" in person, show up on the phone, or through a personal note (try to make it *more* than a casual e-mail).

If you've been paying attention, honey, here is what I hope you got:

- "Showing up" is an important part of being successful—at work, at home, in life in general.

- "Showing up" means meeting people, getting the word out there, letting the right people into your life and letting them know what skills you have.

- "Showing up" means checking your e-mail and other messages, and *being available* to people whom you can benefit, whether in business or personally.

- It is especially important that you "show up" for the people you love most.

- The flip side of "showing up" is knowing when to say "no." (Because saying "yes" indiscriminately will just make you crazy.)

- Sometimes when it's hard or impossible to "show up" in person, you can deftly substitute for your presence by "showing up" on the phone or through a personal note.

CHAPTER THREE

Be Highly Ethical—Even if Nobody Is Watching

"When you trust someone in life and business, the unspoken things are the really important things. Truly, they are."

Leslie, Dottie, and I were huddled around a small table in our office. I had the floor, and the topic was ethics.

"Important conversation," Dottie agreed.

"You quote a price, and the other person just nods, and you have a deep and abiding sense, looking into his eyes, that you will *never* have a problem getting paid the money he will owe you for pitching his book to the major magazines and the networks. And he knows that you will do the best job you possibly can for him.

"That kind of nod. And, on your part, that kind of knowing—that you are dealing with a quality person."

"Oh," said Dottie, "like the man who sent us a check via Fed-Ex last month?"

"Right. He's definitely quality." This was a consultant who was working on a sales technique book and wanted to hire us. We had talked on the phone, and batted around some media approaches and some figures for what our work would cost. I ended the phone conversation by telling him to get back in touch with me when the book was closer to coming out.

Soon afterward a Fed-Ex arrived in my office with a check for 10 percent of the contractual fee I had mentioned. I was a bit surprised, because most people want to "see something" or "have references." They want to know your track record. And that's fine. They have a perfect right. This gentleman, however, apparently had a sense of our quality, dedication, and integrity just by talking with me on the phone. And he got started with us by sending a check that I had not even asked for.

Don't misunderstand me here; we have barked up a few wrong trees in our day. And we no doubt will bark up a few more here and there. But we trust that most people are good and try not to have the wrong people dominate our lives.

My husband, Richard, whose office is down the hall from my own, stopped by briefly to check on our plans for the evening. He had a scowl on his face.

"What's the matter?" Dottie inquired. "You look mad as a bear."

"Aw, people!" Richard exploded. "People who back out on their bills. I can't stand it!"

"Somebody not paying you for equipment you sold?" I asked.

"No, it's not me. It's just happened to another sales rep I see for lunch occasionally—John Boone. He's in electronics. Super nice guy, but possibly too trusting. One of his accounts made six of seven payments on a service project he sold. The work's been done. It's not a piece of equipment, so there's nothing for the company to take back. But the account is ignoring past-due notices. And now John's company is likely to slap him on the wrist pretty hard."

"Ouch!" said Leslie. "That hurts!"

"Whoever that account is," I said, "he represents the kind of person I do not want to work with. He's what I call 'a bad match.' His sense of ethics is bad and working with him doesn't make sense." I seek out people that I can trust in my life—they help me grow a community of friends that value relationships.

When Richard departed, I turned to Dottie and Leslie and warned, "You've got to protect yourself in business. I'll say one thing for boxing; before each match the referee calls the two fighters to the center of the ring and tells them, 'Gentlemen, protect yourselves at all times.' I like that phrase. We should always keep that in mind. That's why checking credit references—and personal references—mandating strict payment terms, and getting the advice of good CPAs and lawyers is important. Otherwise, we're out there flying blind."

-» -» -» -» ⚹ «- «- «- «-

Food arrived from the Chinese takeout down the street, via Charity, our trusty intern. Amid twice-cooked pork, sweet-and-sour shrimp, eggrolls and hot tea, Leslie, Dottie and I settled in to continue our chat about ethics.

"What have ethics got to do with how your life goes, Ceil?" Leslie asked.

"Listen. When I talk to you all about 'creating your good life,' what stands underneath everything is a platform of very fine ethical standards. Without that, the whole process falls apart.

"With so many people around you day by day—husband, children, neighbors, coworkers, clients, etc.—you need to be sure that your life is available for close inspection. In other words, be an open book. No squirreling things away in drawers to be sure nobody sees them. No whispered gossip on the phone. Just be straightforward."

"Remind us of that story about parents and children in a motel room," said Leslie.

"Oh, yeah," Dottie remembered. "It said that when a parent is with a child in a motel room, and the parent takes one of the hotel towels to the car, because the parent really 'needs' it at the moment, that parent is teaching the child that it is OK to steal. It's subtle, but it's there. The old maxim about actions speaking louder than words."

"Right," I approved. "I don't care how much you PREACH about being honest, telling the truth, whatever; it's what you do in your actual life that counts."

I had more I wanted to convey to Dottie and Leslie. After sorting my thoughts for a few seconds, this is what I said to them: "I have a thing about being ethical, even when no one is watching. Do you catch what I'm saying? I mean, even if you could get away with something, and nobody would ever know the difference. But what you are doing is wrong, according to your own standards or your own intuition. Be true to the best of who you are. I know it sounds like a, well, a *platitude*. But hey...."

"Ceil, what about that deal in the restaurant, the piece they did on *Dateline* or was it *20/20?*" Leslie suggested.

"Oh, yeah! One of those shows.... That's the one where they had put a hidden camera in a restaurant, and they had people eating dinner, and when the check came, they had the server deliberately make a mistake on the check. Like, the restaurant charged only $48 when the total should have been $78 or $80. And all the members of the dinner group noticed. It was such an obvious error—something they couldn't miss and would all comment about."

"And none of the five people in the party said anything to the server. They just paid the $48 and left."

"Then, when the camera crew ambushed the group outside, and confronted them with what they had done by paying the amount that was obviously in error, instead of calling it to the server's attention, people were either embarrassed or else they rationalized it. Some wouldn't talk at all. One said something like, 'Well, that restaurant makes plenty of money. They don't need every penny.' And other nonsense like that. Those people thought nobody was watching—and they behaved shamelessly."

"Well, what about people who've gotten into some bad habits—like taking shortcuts with the truth, or not delivering what they promised?" Leslie asked. "What do you say to people like that, Ceil?"

"Maya Angelou, the poet, has a wonderful line that goes something like, 'I did then what I knew how to do, and when I knew better, I did better.'"

Driving home that day after work, I reflected on something I had once read. It was a book that counseled readers to take an inventory of their ethical practices. It really prodded you to look deep within yourself, drudge up your darkest secrets—look at how you are actually running your life.

The author of the book wrote that when he dies he will know he has been successful if he can just overhear what his children say about him, and it's good.

What will my children say about me after I am gone? Will they say, "She had a great business and made a lot of money, but we didn't see her much?" Or will they say, "She was a fine lady who was highly principled and always made time for us in very creative ways?"

Speaking of children, Richard and I went on to have a conversation that evening about how we were doing in our child-rearing challenges. Remembering the talk on ethics I'd had with my coworkers, I said to my husband, "I want to raise two loving, ethical, and caring children. And as far as I can figure out, there's only one way to do that—by example."

"What they see is what they become, huh?"

"The old story about 'Everybody's on the make.' Well, it doesn't wash with me—and that's *not* what I want to pass along to Frank and Elizabeth as their inheritance of values."

Richard nodded in agreement, then went to look for the magazine he'd been reading. I sat alone in the living room, thinking about my life.

When I first started out in television in Miami, I would work on the sets of commercials being shot. Crew members would come down to the set in mobile units, and I would mingle with them. After they had finished shooting a commercial, often a crew would order a whole bunch of supplies that they didn't really need, and put it on the bill for the client for whom they were shooting. That way they'd just stock up on supplies for themselves. A very unethical practice, if not indeed criminal—like stealing money from the client's bank account. I shudder sometimes when I reflect on where I have been, and what I have seen and experienced.

John Izzo, Ph.D., a minister-turned-management consultant and co-author of *Awakening Corporate Soul,* says that when you've "done things right," the feeling you get is "a good tired." What you did may not have been the quickest way, or the easiest path to making money, but the rewards to your soul are priceless.

Living in ethical compromise will mean that your spirit will get all splattered with soot, and deep down, you will no longer respect yourself. Being ethical means treating people like you want to be treated. Make up your mind that you will insist on the highest ethical standards in your life. It makes you feel so good, a feeling money can't buy. And it will be "an estate of pride" you pass down to future generations. If you don't do the right things in life, whatever else you learn in this book won't matter.

If you've been paying attention, honey, here is what I hope you got:

- An honest person will communicate trust to you even without saying a word. There are moments of eye contact, nods, gestures, or even comfortable silences that announce, "You can trust me."

- People who are not trustworthy will give you clues as well, if you pay attention.

- Trust your first impression; your intuition will guide you. You cannot work well with somebody you cannot trust. And don't worry if someone is not "your breed of cat"—not everyone understands the good life.

- High ethical standards are the bedrock of the whole "creating your good life" message I am attempting to convey in this book. If you won't "buy into" the ethics, the rest of my message won't matter—you will lack the peace of soul to enjoy the joyfully simple life. Respect is something you can't buy at any price.

- Strive, therefore, to be the *best*. Treat others with respect, honesty, and integrity. It counts *big*.

CHAPTER FOUR

Pinpoint What Matters Most

"How did I get into this 'simplify your life' kick? Have you ever heard of Elaine St. James?"

"No, I haven't, Ceil. Who is she?"

I was chatting on the phone with Laura, an editor with a West Coast publisher for whom our agency has done some promotion work.

"She wrote a book called *Simplify Your Life.* As soon as I picked it up, I said to myself, '*This* is a book for me!' See, I had been *thinking* about simplification for a long, long time. The only problem was, all the while I was thinking about it, I was acting in a totally different spirit—just giving in to impulse buying and loading up my house with more … *stuff.*"

"Go on, tell me more," Laura said. "I have too much … *stuff* … myself."

"Elaine St. James opens up the world to questions like: 'If nobody was watching, how would you live? Where would you work? How would you dress? What would your house look like?

Your car? Only *you* know, no neighbors, no family, no old friends from college.'"

"Most of us don't think like that, do we Ceil?" Laura put in.

"No, but it's a doable thing. And you feel SOOO much better after you get into it—and out of your compulsive spending and junk-collecting habits."

"Laura, let me tell you what also brought this home to me. When I go on vacation, and I'm in a hotel room, what do I have there? At most I'll have a kitchenette, with a little refrigerator, a microwave, and a sink. I also have a bed, some towels (just a few), TV with cable (because I like movies), and, if I can get it, a view. I have a phone and a hookup for my laptop, so that connects me with the world. Then I have people downstairs who will bring me food if I want it."

"I have basically all the amenities I could desire. I don't start complaining, 'This room is too small, or too limited, or there aren't enough *things* at hand.' On the contrary, I'm quite happy that the room isn't junked up with useless items. When you're on vacation it's apparent that the *world* is your palette."

"Uh-huh, I'm starting to see where you're coming from," Laura said.

"The basics, comfortable, quiet, uncluttered. That's what we hanker for. However, we have a lot of trouble translating our love of the basics to our day-to-day lifestyle at home and at work. We've chosen to be willing prisoners of the marketers of all these products that we *just have to have!*"

A few days later I got a note from Laura. I smiled as I read it. She wrote:

Ceil – That phone chat was a life-changer! I went home and started writing down everything I owned that I really wasn't using or didn't need around or could just as well do without. There was quite a list. I've already had the courage to give away a whole bunch of clothes, unmatched towels, and quite a collection of knick-knacks that were only cluttering up scarce space on bookshelves and on the mantle. It's amazing how much better I feel already—and I think I'm only at the beginning. Love, Laura

What Laura did is what I recommend that *you* do—just as soon as you can: Go and *inventory* what you have in your life. Start with *things*—material possessions—and actually write everything down. (Okay, some of you may never do that. Too many of us have more stuff than we'll ever know what to do with!)

And let's not stop there. Start thinking about a systems-based way of opening up space and time. Develop a structure for what your day entails, figure out how it all works. Then you will clearly see the changes you need to make.

Weekends (usually) are special. They give you that much-needed time off (or time to catch up on things at home).

How do you spend your weekends? Haphazardly? Mindlessly? Or do you put energy into planning weekends that will be fun and fulfilling for you and for the other people in your life?

Now go on to inventory *people*. Who's in your life right now? Put them all down—spouse, boyfriend, children, parents,

41

aunts and uncles, nieces and nephews, neighbors, friends, members of your church community or your fraternal organization. How do you divide your time among them? (Some people have a hard time with this, typically because they had never really thought about it before and at first do not actually know how they spend their days or weeks.)

Last but far from least, what about your relationship with *yourself*? How are you doing in getting to know your own deepest self? How much time do you spend happily *alone*? Do you keep a diary or a journal? If not, would it be a good idea to start one? I have never been a great journal keeper, but I have found that giving your problems a "voice" helps you understand what they are, and is an important step toward solving these issues.

One activity that we do alone is reading. Inventory the periodicals you receive, the books you have bought (at least over the last year). These lists will help you judge whether you need *more* or *better quality* time alone, and whether your reading time is being spent on material that brings you something you need (information, inspiration, humor, hope, and so on).

I used to get three newspapers daily, one local, one national, and one financial. I've cut back to *none*. I get my news online now and through reading a popular news magazine faithfully each week. Then, when something occurs where I want a deeper look, I will buy a newspaper, such as *The New York Times* or *The Washington Post*, specifically in order to read about something that interests me.

This is a good place to mention an important issue: pinpointing what matters most is *a highly individual venture*. If collecting postcards or salt-and-pepper shakers or teapots is a hobby you enjoy, you don't need to feel guilty—you obviously would not make the decision that Laura made. If reading a daily newspaper is a habit you enjoy and never want to break, by all means keep those papers rolling up onto the front porch in time for your morning coffee.

Trekking through supermarkets and loading up a cart with items for our household is definitely *not* the way I want to spend my time. For that kind of shopping I have an errand runner, or else I simply call in an order and have the store deliver to my home. Richard, on the other hand, *loves* grocery shopping. He knows where to find things, and comes up with the most amazing spices and condiments when he shops. (If truth be known, Richard is a gourmet cook; if he had the time he'd probably want his own garden to grow the ingredients for his scrumptious dinners. I wouldn't dream of suggesting that Richard adopt my chosen way of avoiding food stores whenever possible.)

The key idea here is *to find out what is of value to you, and take everything else that needs to be done and figure out a way to have it done for you—and done wonderfully well!* This leads to the subject of *delegation*. This is a key component of organizing the good life. Chapter Seven will focus sharply on this issue. Just tuck this concept away in your mind for the present: you won't be able to "organize the good life" without thoughtful delegation.

"Ceil, the office is going to be forty pounds lighter when I get through here today!"

It was Dottie, calling to me from the corridor where we keep some of our filing cabinets. Dottie is a ruthless purger of things that have outlived their usefulness. When it comes to reducing our office to the bare necessities, Dottie is an absolute genius.

"How do you do it, Dottie?" I called back to her from my office. "You amaze me."

"Thought power!" she fired back. "It takes *energy* to sit down and sift through what you have around you, and *make decisions* about what to let go of, what to keep."

"You're right," I replied. "And the problem many people have is they do not put the mental energy into deciding how to structure their lives. It goes way beyond tossing stuff from cold-storage files. It gets into looking at the way you junk up your time, junk up your relationships, junk up who knows what else."

"People need to *think!*" Dottie finished.

Amen, I said to myself. Think through what's going on in your life, and decide what's important.

Recently, my husband went to Europe and in a glass shop where he was browsing he found these tiny glass ants, red, the size of a real ant. The secret to owning these ants is you have to be able to keep them without losing them. Richard brought them home to our son Frank as a gift. They certainly didn't take up much room in Richard's pocket on the return trip. Frank had to go to school shortly afterward and bring a box of things he felt were interesting to talk about. When I opened his

Ziploc® bag, I found that he was bringing the two tiny ants to school. They were his "show and tell." My son has not learned from us that important things are always big. Important things can be small. It's a reflection of how our family thinks and lives.

Where do you live? Are you happy with that place? Where do you work? Is the work you do in synch with who you are? Is the atmosphere where you work healthy for you? Who's in your circle of friends? Why have you chosen these people?

All of the above are issues that require *thought. Reflection.* As we move through the chapters that follow, you will have an opportunity to zoom in on various aspects of your life that include these and other major issues. You'll have a chance to look around and see if you want to keep things as they are—or live your life differently. Treat this book, then, not as a rigid guide that will give you "all the answers." Treat it as a resource that may provide you with a lot of the "right" questions. The answers, if they are to work, have to come from *you.*

As you read through this book, you may get the impression that I woke up one day and found that the world was my oyster. Well, it wasn't like that. I want to assure you that I've had plenty of ups and downs, of failures as well as success, and it's taken me forty-two years to be able to share the insights I have achieved, insights sometimes gained through difficult experiences. Changing your thinking and habits takes time; be patient with yourself as you try to implement any organizing or simplifying tip.

Before we leave the important subject of pinpointing what matters most, I'd like to say a few words about women trying to "have it all." It is one of the major issues of our times.

I see many people today who feel that their lives are a bit out of control—too much hurly-burly, too much dashing frantically from one place to another, too much clutter, and bills and debts soaring into the stratosphere. Are we all afraid to stop the roller coaster? I believe *having it all* means taking only what we need from the world and giving back the rest.

Over the years I had convinced myself that some hideous monster would rise up and swallow me if I ever got off that roller coaster. At one time I actually believed I'd be homeless if I didn't work day and night. It didn't happen that day, and it hasn't happened since. I now trust that the world is unfolding just like it should and everything will turn out just like it's supposed to.

Some women manage by giving up their high-income (or high-pressure) careers. I know women who have been on the trading floor on Wall Street, and who have given it up to stay home with their children. I know a TV anchorwoman who gave up her prominent spot on the tube to raise her kids. More power to them.

Me? I seem to be cursed. I cannot give up public relations. It is too much a part of who I am. Once a woman spends twenty years developing a skill that produces a high income, how do you coax her into giving it up?

I guess I have way too much energy, too much creativity. So instead of giving up my career, I have been focusing on finding a better way to organize my fast-paced life. It has taken me a long time, more than seven years, to achieve the degree of synchronicity I now enjoy in my life—seven years and many hard lessons learned. But it has been worth the effort.

The bottom line for me now is this: Yes, a woman can have a measure of all three arenas—a healthy love relationship, mothering, and a rewarding career. However, it takes *thought, energy,* and *planning* to make it happen. And my best wish for women reading this is that they will derive from these pages a spark of hope, that they will catch a glimpse of a good life that is *possible.* And be able to find the energy to put it together!

If you've been paying attention, honey, here is what I hope you got:

- If you think you have too much…*stuff*…in your life, you do. Make lists and determine to pare down.

- Ask yourself, "What are the *basics* I need to be comfortable?" If you're daring enough, take a big garbage bag and fill it up with things around you that you really don't need.

- After you've inventoried material possessions, even if you just do so in your mind, reflect on your use of *time*. Next, inventory your *relationships* and notice how much time you allocate to each.

- Go on to chart the time you allocate to *yourself*.

- Inventory the periodicals and books you have been taking and reading over the last year. Make some judgment as to whether what you have been reading has been bringing you something you *need*—information, humor, hope….

- Realize that pinpointing what matters is *very individual*. You don't want your life to be focused on what matters to Celia Rocks, but on what matters to you!

- *Think* deeply about your life and the elements that make up your environment. Be *reflective* as you ponder what is truly important.

- Be assured that for someone to want "to have it all" is quite an ambitious goal—and can be attained only by paying the price of *thinking things through carefully and making good choices regarding relationships, time, and things.*

CHAPTER FIVE

Declutter and Energize Your Environment

"Would you rather be the lady who lives down a quiet street in a cottage that is paid up in full? Or another lady who lives in a very large house on the wealthy side of town and is stuck with a huge mortgage that strains her budget month by month?"

I was sparring with George, a loan officer from a local bank, whom I'd run across at the bookstore. We were both browsing in the personal finance books section.

"Well," George replied. "I guess I'd rather be the one with the paid-up mortgage. That's speaking purely personally, of course. Professionally, most people would recommend diversifying your investments and not paying off your house completely."

"You do see my point, though?" I parried. "What a huge weight off your shoulders—and your mind—to have that mortgage paid off!"

But George was already deeply engrossed in a book that touted the merits of acquiring real estate, and leveraging one property against the next.

I reflected on the situation of our own family. We had done something many American families apparently do not consider:

We had purchased a house that was substantially *under* the loan limits for which Richard and I were qualified. And while we will discuss finances later on in the book, the point I want to make here is that we gave ourselves *less room* to put furniture and store other things. Our house would not have done well loaded to the gills with *possessions*. It called out for being furnished by a few well-chosen items—and no more.

By deliberately choosing a smaller house than we could afford, we also, as a consequence, *chose* to limit what we could buy and put into that house. In our case, *less is more* is a watchword that we live by.

One of my favorite architects is Frank Lloyd Wright, who designed the Fallingwater House in Pennsylvania, a place I love to visit. During tours the guides point out that Wright designed houses so they could hold a minimum of furniture. He actually wanted to *discourage* people from bringing furniture into the house. He would build in bookcases, benches, tables—he was the master of the built-ins.

These are ideas that my husband, Richard, especially appreciates. Our attic in Hickory, for example, was a "no storage" attic. It was always swept clean. There wasn't a single box or piece of junk laying around. Just a nice flat carpeted surface on which the children could play, if they wanted. And in our rooms were all the pieces of furniture that we needed—all comfortable, all in good repair, but just enough to make each room "work."

And when we moved to Pittsburgh, we went from a 2,000-square-foot house to an apartment half the size. What a great challenge it was for us to figure out just what we absolutely needed—and say good-bye to the rest of it. This is probably a terrifying thought to most of you. Connie Cox and Cris Evatt, in their book, *30 Days to a Simpler Life*, make the point, however, that "space is valuable." Owning something means you have to pay a storage fee on it, even if the storage fee is the mortgage you pay by buying, maintaining, or renting enough space to keep it all. It can be liberating to own less, and joyful to be in a smaller space.

-» -» -» -» ꙮ «- «- «- «-

"Organization, my dear, can do more for your life than you would ever imagine!"

I was speaking to my daughter, Elizabeth, on a bright sunshiny Saturday morning in spring. We were, of course, talking about her room. And, at that moment, we were in it. But the point I was making with my daughter was larger than how to pick up her toys or prop up her dolls neatly on the pillow.

"Like what, Mommy? What can it do for you?"

"Organization is the key to success," I pronounced. "Everyone is always looking for a better way to get organized— everyone! If you can manage it, you're way ahead of the game— it helps in school, at work, at home, and it'll help a bunch one day when you have your own children."

"Well, Mommy, I don't think I'm very organized."

"Some people aren't—aren't *naturally* very organized, I mean."

"So what do you do?"

"You know, Elizabeth, I myself am not naturally that organized. I've gotten a lot better. But it's been a real struggle for me. Do you know what, though? I found a solution."

"You did? What is it?"

"Other people. Find people who are really, *really* organized—and let them help organize you. Like your daddy, for example. He is *super* organized. He has helped me get rid of a lot of stuff I did not actually need, and keep other things in very good order. Some people are just born with a knack for this, believe me.

"Your daddy will just walk into a room and rearrange furniture and things, and when he's done, it looks wonderful. Doesn't it?"

"Daddy reorganized *my* room!"

"I know. He's reorganized the whole house."

"But what would we do if we didn't have a daddy that was so good at organization, Mom?"

"We'd find somebody. We'd hire them to come in here and get us organized, that's what."

"Gee, Mom, that'd be cool. So there are enough people out there who know how to do it, and all you need is to find them and get them to work with you?"

"You've got it. What you can't do yourself, find somebody who's good in that area—and hire them."

As I've mentioned, I grew up in Miami, and where I lived, it was mostly about acquiring "stuff." So I followed suit. By the time I met Richard I was immersed in "stuff." I had boxes and boxes of "stuff." Well, all this stuff comes from one phenomenon: shopping.

So a key to cutting down on the "stuff" that is choking you is to rein in your mania for shopping. There's no better place to start reorganizing your life than to look at how you shop, and make improvements.

A man I spotted in a gift shop one day, with his little boy in tow, taught me a lesson. The boy would go up to this or that trinket, and say, "Can we get ... ?" or "Could I have ... ?" And the man would go, "Junk."

On and on it went. The little boy would say, "Oh, look, Dad! Look at that!"

And his father would respond, "Junk!"

Pretty soon the boy picked up on it. He began pointing out things to his Dad in the store and saying, "Junk."

Now I am not, of course, here to condemn the manufacturing and selling of gift items. It's an important industry. But what we all have to do is become much more discriminating about what we acquire and try to squeeze into our houses and our offices. Because whatever eventually doesn't "fit" is going to clutter up your open space, which your soul needs to breathe.

If you think you just "have to" buy something you see in a store today, stop and tell yourself, "It'll probably be there tomorrow," or "If I keep looking, I'll find something I like even better."

Going cold turkey from shopping is not the easiest thing to do. I realize that for some people, it's virtually their favorite hobby. I can remember when going to the mall was an entire day's event, like playing golf or visiting a museum. In fact, when I was pregnant I used to walk in the mall as my exercise. So when I started to declutter my environment, the shopping urge would sometimes come upon me. So what did I do? I took a one-hundred dollar bill and went to the big Wal-Mart near my house. I would spend the $100 on the goofiest trinkets I could find. It would take me a good two hours to buy all the stuff, go through checkout, and dump it in my car. On the way out of the parking lot I would come upon the big blue Goodwill trailer, and I'd drop off everything I had just bought. For you it may be a little different scenario. You may shop just to buy presents for your children's teachers, your landlord, or a friend or neighbor. Whatever—just don't bring it home!

As for myself, I don't buy anything (other than food products or common household items, like paper towels) on a first-look basis anymore. In other words, I have weaned myself from impulse buying. Unless I go home and think about it overnight, I'm probably not going to buy it.

In fact, I have trained myself to walk through stores as if I were walking through a museum. And a museum is for looking. You don't go through a museum and then say to the custodian, "I'll take the dinosaur eggs."

I've adopted the same attitude toward making quick decisions. I no longer hesitate to say, "You know what? I'm going to have to think about that. Let me get back to you tomorrow." That is such a great answer. It won't keep you from giving to causes in which you truly believe. It will prevent you from doling out your money—or time—indiscriminately.

-» -» -» -» ❧ «- «- «- «-

"Ceil, I think I've got a problem, and I hope you can help."
It was Megan, another member of my fine team at Rocks-
Del Iart Public Relations. She had caught me on my cell phone,
just as I was heading out with Frank and Elizabeth for an ice-
cream treat at Baskin-Robbins.

"Business or personal, Megan?"

"Mostly personal, I guess. I've had this girlfriend from college who has just been sort of a hanger-on. She's someone that
has stayed around here after her marriage ended a few years ago,
even though most of her friends and family are back in her
hometown in eastern North Carolina. I may be one of the few
people she knows really well in this area."

"So what's the problem?"

"Well, she calls me to complain about her life. A lot. I
mean, she's taken to calling me about things that she should
have under control. When we get together, it's more of the
same. I'd like to help, but I've really don't know if I can. I know
you've talked before about something you call 'minimizing the
effects of negativity on your life.' Just what is that? And how
do you do it?

"Megan, I have very strong feelings on this subject. I
believe that you should keep your life focused on the positives
as much as possible. We all have problems, but we need to take
positive action instead of complaining.

Therefore, when people around you start loading you down with negatives, or negative behavior, you have to be good to yourself and find ways to reduce the effects of other people's 'unhealthy vibes.'

"One good way, of course, is to spend more time around people who have a positive effect on you. Seek people out that make you feel good about yourself and about what you are doing in life. But I realize that you cannot simply avoid people who are prone to complain about things or those who are not in the same 'place' as you."

"So how do you handle a relationship with people like that?"

"When your complaining friend calls, you simply say, 'I've decided I'm going to focus on the positives. Let's talk about what we have to be grateful for and how we can make things better. Let's take positive action.

"And let's start now."

So what I told Megan I want to be sure you get, too. You may need a real awakening on this point, because one way that some people clutter up their life, and wreck their organization, is by letting the constant complainers and people who are not on the joyful road to a peaceful and organized life take up their time. That process also fills the soul with negative, or poisonous, matter.

Take a moment right now, if you would, and jot down people or situations in your life that tend to drag you in a negative direction.

Next, make a firm resolution that you are going to change the way you handle these people. You are going to put some limits on how much of their tales of woe you will allow yourself to listen to. I don't believe in confronting these sorts of situation by telling someone point blank, "You can't be my friend anymore." You can, however, let them know that their actions or behaviors are an intrusion on your personal peace.

What I have found is that these negative people will just start reducing their assault on your goodwill, if you are firm with them. They may find someone else who is more willing to let them spout off, or they may actually decide to stop whining so much. People change, life is long. I am just asking you to spend your precious time right now on people who want to help you live a good life. Surround yourself, in other words, with positive people. You'll thus allow less room for negativity.

If you've been paying attention, honey, here is what I hope you got:

- The smaller the dwelling you can live in comfortably, the less "stuff" you'll be able to fit in. Consider this a benefit.

- Keep what you store to the bare minimum. If something stays in long-term storage and out of use, ask yourself, "Why am I holding onto this?" Determinedly throw out or give away what you do not need.

- Organization is the key to success—at home, at school, at work, when traveling—everywhere!

- If you are not "good" at organization, find someone who is—and pay him or her to help you. It's easy to find people who have a knack for getting others organized.

- Ruthlessly rein in your shopping for nonconsumables (furniture, gadgets, decorative pieces).

- When someone solicits you to buy something, say, "I'll have to think it over." Then do so. Buy only upon reflection for at least a day or two.

- Learn how to minimize the effect of people who whine and complain constantly, who don't share your values, or who try to drag you into a negative mode. Focus your life on the positives.

- To the degree possible, arrange your world so that the chemistry between you, your clients/customers, and workplace associates is positive and healthy.

CHAPTER SIX

Choose Quality

My friend and neighbor, Suzanne, and I were sipping cappuccino at Starbucks, comparing notes on husbands. Suzanne is married to Allen, the fellow who asked about the incorporate-by-mail offer. Remember him?

"Allen is so ... how shall I put it? 'Cost conscious.' He can't *stand* paying full price for anything. If it isn't on sale, forget it!" Suzanne said. "I guess he does end up saving us money, but really, he's so *obsessed* ... ."

"Being cost conscious is good. But maybe he doesn't see the long term. If you're always looking for a bargain, you may also end up buying stuff that is cheap, meaning not made very well," I rejoined. "I used to be more like Allen, but I've gotten less so since developing a life with Richard."

"Richard always presents himself so ... what? Right for the occasion, I guess."

"I know," I told Suzanne, "but he doesn't shop very often. And he buys only what he needs, but he pays whatever it takes to get quality. Did I ever tell you the story of the $750 coat he bought me years ago?"

"That all-time classic coat you wear to all the events?"

"That's the one."

"Something about an argument you and Richard had, wasn't it?"

"Yes. It was ten years ago. We went into a Burberry of London store together, and I needed a coat. Nothing too warm, just a coat to wear when I traveled on business—you know, into the plane, off the plane, into a taxi, and out into a hotel. I was looking at these nice and, I thought, pricey-enough coats, when Richard came down an aisle in the store with this gorgeous coat with a huge price tag.

"'What, are you CRAZY!?!,' I scolded him. I could go down to Burdine's and get myself a nice coat for maybe $125."

"'Not like this one you can't,' he came back at me. And in the end he talked me into getting it. Do you know, Suzanne, I've been wearing that coat for many, many years now. I've worn it to meetings, I've worn it to Europe, it's been everywhere, and it never, ever has made me look anything but wonderful. This is a coat that will never go out of style. I have it cleaned, and it looks brand new. If I need to replace the lining or the belt, I can do it; the company still sells all the accessories for this coat."

"Ceil, I bet I've paid more than $750 for coats over the last ten years myself, just buying one after another and having them wear out or go out of style or just getting tired of them."

"There are lots of women who do just as you have done, and who would never dream of spending so much on a coat. The economics, however, favor quality, long-lastingness—not fashions that shift with every new calendar year. It's just that very few people think that way. But they *should*."

We paid for our cappuccino and I grabbed a box of mints. I waved Suzanne off in her car and drove back to my office—with a brief stop at my favorite park.

-» -» -» -» ❦ «- «- «- «-

Once ensconced on a bench in a bucolic downtown park, I let my mind drift back to other purchases I had made—many of them at Richard's urging: a Rolex watch, hairdos at upscale salons in New York and abroad so that I would always look and feel wonderful, top-of-the line equipment for my office. I thought of how good those few well-chosen quality items had been for the kind of life I lead, that of an on-the-go woman business owner and marketer. My car itself, now parked under a spreading maple nearby, provided me with other reflections on quality—and *security*.

Ahh ... nothing like *always* driving a new car. That's why I lease. The car is kept in excellent condition, so that I minimize the chance of breaking down on some lonely highway at night. You can't be a queen if you don't feel safe. So...protect yourself! And then there are always new security features every year. In the latest model the dealer leased me, there is a side airbag. I feel much safer than with only one airbag under the steering wheel.

Mechanically, everything is under full warranty. I never have to pay a repair bill on my car. *Never!* Therefore, wherever I am in my car, I feel very safe and very secure.

Whether you lease or buy a car, you want to make sure that you keep it well maintained, clean, and looking good so that you'll feel good when you drive it.

I glanced down at my handbag, resting beside me on the bench, and was reminded of a whole sequence of events. I had bought the predecessor to this bag, a Feragamo purse, at Saks Fifth Avenue in New York about five years ago. It's probably the most expensive purse I've ever bought; I think I paid something like $500 for it. Well, recently that purse's latch broke. Richard was then on the verge of a trip to New York, so he took the purse with him and went into Saks Fifth Avenue with it. The Saks people said, "You know, Farragamo doesn't make this purse anymore, but it was about a $490 purse. What if we just credit your account for half the price?" So they took back the purse and gave me a credit for $250. Then they sent me a card thanking me for doing business with Saks Fifth Avenue and inviting me to stop by next time I would be coming to New York and see their new collection of Farragamo products. The letter was personalized and signed by the woman in charge of Farragamo's line at Saks.

So I did stop by on my next trip to the big city, applied my credit, and came home with the purse I now carry. Even though it's expensive it's much cheaper in the long run because it lasts so long and looks so good. And as you can imagine, I don't have a whole bunch of cheap purses cluttering up my closet. The whole experience of being able to shop at Saks and carry a Faragamo purse just makes me feel incredibly affluent. And really I don't qualify as a bona fide member of America's wealthy set, but because of my insistence on quality, I share in many features of the upper-bracket lifestyle.

Back in the office, I surveyed my working atmosphere. Everything was quality: high-speed computer, the laser printer, my solid maplewood desk, and the ergonomic chair I had bought upon the recommendation of an expert. On my walls hung some favorite paintings and graphic designs.

Anyone who doesn't have his or her office set up *just* the way he or she wants is missing out *big time*. Your office is where you earn your living, where you spend between one quarter and one third of your life every week. And yet I know people who put considerably more attention into furnishing their living room than they do into furnishing their work space.

Leslie poked her head in.

"Ceil, I just have to tell you: I finally bought the really terrific black dress I've always wanted. You know how you're always preaching 'quality'? Well, I decided you were absolutely right. I have a ton of little black dresses in my closet, but for this party I went to last weekend, I felt like I had to go out and buy another one. None of those black dresses I had were exactly right; they'd all been bought 'on sale,' and in a moment when I was worrying much more about cost than about quality. And, literally, by the time you buy four *wrong* dresses, you can afford to buy one really great dress."

"Good for you," I told her. "You're catching the right spirit. Now give me a minute; I have to book a flight."

Booking flights is something I do myself. Because an airplane trip can be a disaster if you don't allow yourself enough time, if the plane is at all uncomfortable, if you arrive in a city at rush hour—there are a dozen things to check. I'm proud to be my own executive secretary for making reservations. I dialed the number.

"US Airlines Reservations, this is Rebecca, how may I help you?"

"Rebecca, this is Celia Rocks. I need to book a flight from Charlotte, North Carolina, to Chicago, on coach, for June 1, returning June 4. What flight times do you have?"

"We have departures at 6:55 a.m., 9:43 a.m., 1 p.m., and 4:55 p.m."

"Let's see, Chicago is one hour behind Eastern time, correct?"

"Right."

"Well, could you give me the arrival times?

Yes, those would be departing Charlotte at 6:55 a.m., arriving Chicago-O'Hare at 7:20 a.m.; departing Charlotte at 9:43 a.m., arriving Chicago-Midway at 10:15 a.m.; departing Charlotte at 1 p.m., arriving Chicago-O'Hare at 1:20 p.m.; and departing Charlotte at 4:55 p.m., arriving Chicago-O'Hare at 5:15 p.m.

"What's the traffic like on the expressways at 7:30 a.m. and 5:30 p.m.?"

"Actually, it's usually pretty bad. Do you want to aim for one of the other two flights?"

"Yes, I think so. Now your 9:43 a.m. goes into Midway. I've never been to that airport. What's it like? Is it just as easy to get to the Loop as it is from O'Hare?"

"Oh, Midway's nice. Much cozier than O'Hare. And it's so easy to get a taxi. It's not such a long walk from your plane to the taxi line. And I think it's even easier to get downtown from Midway than it is from O'Hare. It's a shorter ride, and traffic is not likely to be as congested." (Please note: not all reps will know about different airports. Don't settle for inadequate customer service; rather, ask to speak to a supervisor.)

"Well let's do that flight then. That'll give me plenty of the day for meetings. What kind of aircraft do you have going into Midway?"

"It's a 737. I think you'll like ... ."

"That'll be fine. Can I have an aisle seat?"

"Seat selection for that flight is normally handled at the gate. So just be sure to show up early enough to secure the seat you prefer."

"How early should I be there?"

"I would say an hour before the flight ought to be fine."

"Thank you, Rebecca. I'm ready to take down my confirmation number."

You will find plenty of other occasions in your work life to take over the secretarial reins and make sure you organize events or situations to ensure a quality result. Don't delegate the wrong things. I still book all my flights and hotels because traveling is something I do well.

-» -» -» -» ⚡ «- «- «- «-

Many of my ideas about quality I learned from my husband Richard. He has always had a thing about making me feel as comfortable, and as well cared for, as possible. Often, because he loves being surrounded by quality, this translates into the notion of "spend whatever it takes."

Some of you may be shaking your heads and asking, "What if I don't want the best of everything? What if I like driving an older car, for instance?"

And I say, "Fine." If you absolutely love driving an older car, then drive one. Don't drive an older car because you're willing to treat yourself badly—in other words, you'd ideally like to drive a new Camry, but you're driving a nine-year-old Chevy coupe because you just have never gotten your act together.

I have a friend who is a multimillionaire. He drives an old Impala. He loves it because he is inconspicuous with it. He can park it anywhere; he leaves it at the airport when he takes a flight. He never worries about someone stealing the car, or trying to hit up on him as a rich guy; he just blends in with the crowd, and he likes that.

Technology is a big thing with me. All members of the Rocks-DeHart team have offices in their homes. This was a decision we made as a group, that they would basically work at home as much as they liked and at the office whenever that was appropriate. We always get together, nonetheless, because we never want to lose that critical face-to-face contact. For instance, we would meet once or twice a week for planning sessions. (Of course, we are in and out of the main office more often than that, but you get the idea.) Leslie, Megan, and Dottie are all high achievers, and to maximize their output, we buy the best equipment we can find—the best computers, the best fax machines. When we buy pens, we don't just get the ten-pack for $4.99. We buy really nice pens so that when each of us writes a personal note on behalf of the company, she gets to write it with elegance, and feel good about it.

People today are hungry for quality. When they find it, they will refer others to your firm. People will remember it when they experience it. Quality can *never* get you in trouble.

If you've been paying attention, honey, here is what I hope you got:

- It's good to be cost conscious, but never let it get in the way of buying *quality*.

- *Quality* clothing, equipment, or whatever else will pay for itself over time, as it will outlast and outperform your lesser purchases. If you can't afford the best of everything, try buying the best of *one* thing and add to it as time goes on.

- Owning quality items will help you feel better about yourself—in some cases, more secure or even safer.

- Your life will be much more comfortable day by day if you put the emphasis on quality and quality planning, not only for material goods but also for services, such as air travel.

- Quality is an individual lifestyle choice. If you buy something second-hand or older, let it be because that is the item you want (e.g., such as an old set of encyclopedias), not because you are scrimping or because you are not treating yourself well.

- Quality is contagious. Once you exhibit a predilection for quality, those around you at home and at work are likely to emulate you. You will thus help to create an atmosphere of quality in both of these important life spaces. And junk will be hard to hide!

CHAPTER SEVEN

Delegate Everything You Can—And Hire the Best!

"Thanks so much for having Elizabeth and Frank over to play with Joy and Bobby," I said as my friend Suzanne opened the door of the English Tudor she shares with her husband Allen and their happy brood.

"Ceil, come on in and sit a few minutes. The kids are fine ...."

"Yeah, we're fine, Mom!" said Frank as he scored more points in the computer game the four of them were playing in the family room.

"Well...."

"Coffee's on, or I can make tea. We also have the usual array of orange juice, ginger ale, white wine, whatever."

"Decaf if you have it, or else tea would be fine."

"Tea it is then; we're out of decaf."

We settled into the warmly upholstered chairs on Suzanne's sun porch. Besides being a Mom, Suzanne shoulders some major-league responsibilities as a pharmacist and store manager. By her intent look I could tell already that Suzanne had an agenda for our chat. I had guessed right, I knew, when she began: "Ceil, I wanted to talk to you about your errand runner. What's her name? Nickie? How does it work? And how do you find somebody good?"

"Yes, Nickie. She comes before her classes at Duquesne University, say, 8:30 a.m. I stop whatever I'm doing and spend about fifteen minutes with her going over a list of errands for the day. It varies a lot from day to day. It might involve delivering or picking up dry cleaning, and bringing the clean clothes home and arranging them in their proper places. Then she might take my car from my office parking space, put it through the car wash, fill it with gas, check the oil. She may also pick up an order at the pharmacy and put the medicine in the medicine cabinet. Or she may drop off film to be processed, shoes to be cleaned and shined, or any one of a whole laundry list of errands."

"Wow! That would certainly free up a lot of time, wouldn't it?"

"It does. And since my hours are much better spent running my business and having quality time with Richard and Frank and Elizabeth, I come out way ahead."

"What do you pay Nickie?"

"Ten dollars an hour, and she's worth every penny. I may have her work nine hours a week—more or less. That comes to $90. I save many hours a week by having Nickie run errands for me, and I charge $100 an hour for my services, so, as you can see, I'm actually *making* money by hiring my runner. Besides, running errands wears me out."

"This sounds as if you've learned to run your home like a small business—hiring good people, delegating tasks, coaching the employees, and so forth."

"You've got it. And it works, too!"

"How does Nickie like this kind of job?"

"You'd have to ask *her* to get her truest answer. But I can tell you that in general college students would much prefer being an errand runner to working at the mall or waiting tables."

"How do you find a good errand runner—someone you can trust with a key to your house?"

"Oh, I found Nickie through a friend of mine. Nickie was a roommate of a girl who had been babysitting for my friend, and doing a good job, for a couple of years. You'd be surprised how many good people you can find if you look around, and ask friends and relatives whom they would recommend."

"Well, Ceil, you've already got me hooked on delegating some of the yardwork, because, as you may recall, I hired a fellow on your say-so last spring. And he's been terrific for our yard. I guess I'm going to have to find somebody like Nickie. Maybe she has a friend … ?"

"Great idea! Any friend of Nickie's would already be someone you can probably trust. I'll ask Nickie if she knows anyone who might be available."

"It would sure save me a lot of energy on days when I have to work overtime at the pharmacy."

"You're on. I'll help you look for someone. All right, you guys, Frank, Elizabeth, let's go home—I think Daddy's doing one of his gourmet suppers for us!"

Driving home with the kids buckled into their seatbelts in back, I started to savor the flavorful aromas of Richard's cooking. He must be the prince of sauces. And he knows just where to find all the right spices and garnishes. Shopping and cooking are two things I love to delegate—and Richard loves to do himself. When he's away on trips for his business, I delegate much of the grocery shopping to an errand runner, or else just have the store put together an order for me and deliver it to the house.

When Richard's home, I know enough to shut down that delegated service and let him do his thing.

-»> -»> -»> -»> ✸ «- «- «- «-

Delegation is a flexible system. My client, Jennifer White, always said, "Do what you're brilliant at. And write a check for everything else."

One of the most interesting things to me is that if you get the delegation process down, and rolling along smoothly, then everything else in your life will work better. Be the CEO—of your life! You now really value your time, and the time of others in your family and of those who work for you (or with you).

I actually got into delegating years ago when I was growing up in Miami. That city has a very sizable Cuban community. You haven't really eaten until you've had a good Cuban meal. Latin people in general, in my opinion, are some of the best cooks in the world. In any case, in Miami there is a common practice called "Cantina." This is a service that delivers home-cooked Cuban meals to your doorstep. I think this is common in much of Latin America, where commercial places cook big pots of paella and other such dishes that lend themselves to being divided into many servings.

So I got into the habit in Miami of ordering from one of these services, and they would deliver a meal to my apartment. It was always *delicious!* And not expensive—maybe $8 per meal, and cheaper if you order by the week or the month. I thought to myself, "My God, why would somebody get off work, go to the grocery store, buy the food, bring it home, wash it, cook it—unless, of course, that's what you enjoy doing on an everyday basis."

That's when I realized that many Americans do not realize how many wonderful services are available to them, especially in metropolitan areas. It dawned on me that many people simply do not have a grip on delegation with regard to organizing their lives. They think they have to "do it all" *themselves.*

After I started using Cantinas, I thought of other ways people could act as my "minibutlers." I found a dry cleaner that would pick up at my home and deliver clean clothes back to my home, or to my office, in plastic bags. They come on Monday and pick up and return with the clothes on hangers on Thursday.

Pharmacies, some grocery stores, and other retail establishments will also deliver. So ask, and you may be surprised to find you can save yourself quite a few trips.

If you fill out a few forms, your local bank will arrange direct deposit of your paycheck. This will free you from driving to the bank, looking for a parking space, waiting in line, and so forth just to get your money into the bank. In today's technological world, it's funny to me how people will still wait in line to feel the money in their hands.

Looking back on my earlier life, I realize that for quite a while I had myself fooled: I actually believed that I *enjoyed* running my own errands, I had done them for so long. What I now know is that as an independent business woman and homemaker, I do need to make connections with the people who act as my "vendors." I need to meet the manager at the dry cleaners; I need to know the pharmacist, the people at the post office, etc. So I do get to know those people. However, I don't need to see them all the time. Therefore, I can send my errand runner around, and she represents me, and they still know me as the customer. That is truly the one-two of how to effectively delegate: Get to know the vendors yourself, then delegate the dropoffs and pickups.

You'll have a more personal relationship with some vendors than with others. Remember Roy, my yardman in Hickory? He used to ring my doorbell once in a while just to say "hello" and drop off his bill. It was a small town, so Roy and I did the small-town "thing": we sat down and chatted for a few minutes. I would write his check and praise him for the great job he did with our grass, shrubs, and flower gardens. He would walk away with a very big smile on his face. That left me with a smile, too.

It's a two-way street once you take time to smell the roses and notice your fellow human beings.

This kind of interaction works for me just as well in Pittsburgh, and it can work for you, too, whatever the size of the city or town in which you live.

-» -» -» -» ⚘ «- «- «- «-

"Hi, Ceil, smell good?"

It was Richard greeting me by poking his head out of the kitchen in our apartment.

"Terrific! What have you got on?"

"Oh, it's just a little lobster and crab concoction I swiped from a chef on the Connecticut coast last time I was up around Mystic Seaport."

"Tell me, though: How do you ever manage to keep the kitchen so clean while you're tossing these delicacies together?"

"Cook and clean, clean and cook; keep your counter polished like a whistle. You don't want anything to contaminate the food."

"You're amazing, you know that?"

"I sent the maid home when I got here. She was just about to dust the living room."

"Richard, I know you're a fanatic for dusting. But geez, you could have at least let her do her job."

"Well, we all have our obsessions. And dusting is one of mine."

"You and I sure part company there. I think that any professional who hasn't hired a housekeeper is out of his or her mind. I mean there are people like *you*, Richard, people who actually *enjoy* cleaning a house. Then, you know, you pay the housekeeper a little bit more than he or she asks for—and you get a fabulous cleaning job."

"You mean if I strike out in heavy equipment, I could always make it as a housekeeper?"

"Very funny. When's dinner?"

Richard gave me his little laugh that said, "Whenever the sauce is just right, that's when," and I ambled down to the family room with a cool drink in hand. We keep our family scrapbook down there, and it gave me great pleasure to open it and leaf through the pages. There, laid out in the most stunning order and elegance, was our family history through pictures and memorabilia. Talk about a brilliant stroke of delegation!

Let me fill you in on what happened. About two years ago I realized that the pictures I had of my family were in a hopeless jumble—as is the case in many families. I had all these pictures stuffed into twenty-five boxes. Someone told me about a woman who was a specialist at helping people do scrapbooks. She was selling the empty books and giving classes on how to accomplish a great scrapbook. I wanted even more. I wanted her to actually *do* our scrapbook for us.

"How much would you charge?" I asked her.

"Oh, you don't want to do that," she replied. "It would cost you too much. It would take me three weeks to put all your pictures in scrapbooks. Besides, even the empty scrapbooks themselves that we have to offer are expensive enough—they have special acid-proof paper and are guaranteed for 100 years. And when I do a scrapbook, everything is perfectly placed and labeled, with many aesthetic touches."

BINGO! I had found a way to get the best scrapbooks in the world. I can find the best of anything. It's one of my talents. So I said to her, "No, I really want to know how much it would cost to have you put all our pictures into a scrapbook." She gave me an outrageous figure—something like $1,500, and I said, "Done!"

Now we have one of the world's truly gorgeous scrapbooks. And what a treasure it is! A work of art! Fifteen hundred dollars may seem like an awful lot of money to spend on a scrapbook, but what else do you have that's more precious than memories of your family at every stage of your growth together? Believe me, if my house was on fire and I could grab only one physical item, it would be the family photos in those scrapbooks. When my kids get married, each one will get a scrapbook.

I leaned back and started to daydream a bit. Suddenly, I imagined that I saw a list appearing on our living room wall. It was something I had been trying to get my mind around, that list, so that I could present it to you in this book. And there it was "written on the wall," a list of "everything you can delegate" if you really want to organize the good life:

- Cleaning your house.
- Doing your laundry so that it is washed, dried, ironed, folded, and put into the right drawers.

- Upgrading software on your computer.
- Reorganizing your clothes drawers so that everything is folded neatly and in "the right place."
- Taking your dog to be groomed.
- Baking a dish for you to take to a get-together.
- Sorting your children's toys into categories and bins with labels.
- Putting gas in your car.
- Washing your car.
- Taking your car for an oil change and a checkup.
- Tutoring your children in reading—or math.
- Changing batteries in appliances such as smoke detectors and flashlights.
- Cutting the grass.
- Raking leaves.
- Dropping off clothes to be cleaned or repaired.
- Reorganizing your kitchen to make it more efficient.
- Balancing your personal checkbook.
- Organizing your tax files.
- Taking special letters and packages to the post office.
- Dropping off film to be developed—and retrieving the prints and negatives, and then labeling them and putting them in albums.
- Filing health insurance.
- Doing holiday and birthday gift shopping and wrapping.
- Entering on your computer a simple database of all of

your personal and professional contacts.

- Preparing a dinner and leaving it on the stove to be heated up later in the day.

I think there's something to be said for not being in the grocery store unless you *want* to be there. I also think you can hire someone to go pick up dinner for you and your family. I've had students come to my office and vacuum and dust, and water the plants.

I have an accountant, but I work with him only once a year when he's about to do our taxes. Otherwise, I rely on a weekly bookkeeper. She comes into the office, updates everything—including the checkbook—files all our financial reports, and sends in the worker's comp and unemployment insurance checks. I basically have everything done for me that I can—especially everything I don't particularly enjoy doing or am not very good at doing.

You won't always get the quality you may want the first time you hire a runner or some other independent contractor. Gradually, however, you can find just the right people—people you can trust, people who are good at what you've asked them to do, even people who take great pleasure in things that might bore you or make you feel you were not spending your time well. There are indeed people who are qualified to do important things regarding your work better than you could do them yourself. Perhaps you run a successful company, but maybe you should never be allowed to do the filing. When you find the right people, pay them well. They are worth it and will free you up to get paid well at what you are great at.

And with that thought, I'm going to end this chapter. A scrumptious lobster and crab dinner is now ready, Richard has just announced, and my job is to round up Frank and Elizabeth and get them to the table.

If you've been paying attention, honey, here is what I hope you got:

- You don't have to "do it all." Delegation is the key to being an effective CEO of your life—both at home and at work.

- An errand runner at a relatively modest hourly rate can free up time for you to be good at what you do professionally, and generate more revenue in the process.

- The list of tasks that you can effectively delegate is long. Review the sample list on page 78 and 79. Realize that you can add many other tasks to that list.

- Delegation is a flexible system. There may be occasions when you, or someone else in your family, may want to take back some work from your "delegates" and handle it personally.

- Banks, pharmacies, supermarkets, office supply outlets, and many other institutions and stores have services to save you time. Check with each to see how they can help, whether through "direct deposits" at the bank, or pickup and delivery services at the dry cleaners, or home delivery by stores.

- While you can delegate many pickups and deliveries, and such things as oil or tire changes, to an errand runner, you as the customer should get to know all your vendors *personally*. Then let your errand runner represent you to each of them.

- If you check with family, friends, neighbors, coworkers, and so forth, you will be amazed to see how many qualified and trustworthy people you can find to whom you can delegate one or more tasks.

- You may not always find the best person on the first try, but you can gradually upgrade the quality of your "delegates." Aim for the best you can find. Quality will prove itself—and pay for itself.

CHAPTER EIGHT

Give Privileged Time to Those You Love

"Oh, Wow, Frank! Great sound!" my son's violin teacher, Paula, exclaimed. The sunlight pouring through the windows of the Pittsburgh Music Academy added its own magical touch to the moment.

Frank lowered his instrument from his shoulder and beamed. Elizabeth, waiting her turn, seemed to be wondering if she would do as well as her brother. I smiled at her to let her know, "You can get a big compliment from your teacher, too. I believe in you."

"Paula" I remarked, "I read in *Time* magazine recently that music expands the brain, opens up a whole cavity in the brain for learning."

"Yes, I saw that," she replied. "And violin and piano are the surest ways to open up that channel, according to that piece."

It's good we're doing this, I thought, spending some of our money on violin lessons for our children instead of a bigger mortgage or trinkets that we don't really need. And more than that, I rejoiced that I had been able to arrange my schedule to be part of Frank and Elizabeth's lesson.

It hadn't always been this way. I had to come to the realization that taking my children to their violin lessons every week was really "showing up" for them. Everybody talks about getting "quality time" with their children. Well, it isn't that easy to do. Sometimes it requires rearranging your work life. And in this particular instance, that's exactly what I had done. I arrange my schedule so that I stop by my children's school and volunteer an hour's time helping Elizabeth's teachers. Then I take both Frank and Elizabeth to their violin lessons.

Although I do not play violin at all myself, I am nonethless the one who must supervise their practices at home. And since I've organized my life to be present at their lessons, I have been immensely more effective working with them during their practice sessions.

Children can feel whether you are loving them through a donation of time and attention—or not. It's not that you have to be there every moment. But their progress in school is important, and so you need to get to know each of their teachers. And what they choose to do *after* school is important also. I don't make them all, but I try to get to as many of my son's baseball games as I can. Elizabeth has been a bit hesitant about getting into sports, but whatever she eventually elects to do, I will follow her and her team.

At home we eat together as a family as much as possible. Richard, of course, has to be away frequently to succeed in his business. When he is home with us, however, he makes sure we eat together and talk. Life is good at the family dinner table.

After Elizabeth had indeed proven herself on her assigned violin piece for the week, we packed up the instruments and headed home.

-»→ -» -» -» ✶ «- «- «- «-

As you can tell already, I believe strongly in being a mother—a loving, encouraging, and *present* mother, all the while carrying on what has to be called "a high-powered career." Once again, it is not easy, but it *is* possible.

I read a book once about sequencing. I tried to find it again to give to friends and found that it was out of print. Let me just paraphrase what I remember from this book. The author explains that you will have between seventy and eighty years of life. So let's say you divide your life into periods of ten years. For a woman, this author suggests, the period between a mother being thirty-five and forty-five years old might be the sequence "at home." My own sense in reading this was that the author had it right; this period truly ought to be spent at home, because the children would be in their prime formative years.

My fondest hope for myself and my family during this period of my life was that I could indeed take time off from working and concentrate on childrearing. By then, however, I had become way too immersed in my profession. Once you teach a man to shave, it is hard to take his razor away from him. Same with a woman whom you allow to become skilled in something she truly loves. It's very hard to take that away from her. And so we look for compromises—the kind I am outlining for you in this book. Ways of making our irrational choices work.

Part of the way I make my life work is to surround myself with people who are smarter than me. I'm pretty smart, but everyone around me is even smarter. I married a smart man, Richard, and I have hired extremely smart people for my public relations business—people like Dottie who eventually became my partner, and Leslie, and Megan. I have set my children up with lessons with a sensitive and very talented violin teacher, and a reading tutor of similar qualities. Whenever I come upon a problem to be solved or a service that must be provided, I look for the best and sharpest people I can find.

All of this translates into providing a high-quality atmosphere for my husband, our children, and myself. In other words, choosing quality is a way of being loving.

That evening, as we gathered around the table for supper, Richard, as always, had questions for Frank and Elizabeth.

"What happened with violin today? What are you learning?"

"I played the first bars of 'Go Tell Aunt Rhody,'" Frank exuded.

"Ms. Zimmerman said, 'Wow, Great sound!' after he played," Elizabeth chimed in.

"And what did *you* play, Elizabeth?"

"I'm still learning to do 'Twinkle, Twinkle, Little Star' right, but she said today I played *much* better than ever before," Elizabeth replied.

"And how about your reading lessons?"

"We're learning to take parts in a play, and read really *dramatically,*" Frank said.

"Yeah, it's real good. It's this scene from a play," Elizabeth picked up. "Everybody is gathered around the dinner table, and nobody is noticing each other very much. And the ghost who comes back to see the family is sooo sad 'cause people who are supposed to be family are just thinking about their own stuff instead of loving each other."

"And we don't do that, I hope?"

"No, when we eat together, we notice each other," Frank said. "We might not always agree, but we sure do *talk.*"

From there we plunged into a discussion of our next trip as a family to New York City. Richard and I are firm believers in traveling together with our children. Frank and Elizabeth have been all over with us—to Washington, to New York, to Paris and Milan, to Buenos Aires, the Cayman Islands, and numerous other cities and towns. When we're in New York together I like to take them to Tiffany's to see the Tiffany diamond, which is, well, huge.

I say to them, "I just want you to know that there are diamonds that big and that's what they look like." I tell them this not so much that when they see a really nice diamond, they'll recognize it, but more because this kind of education opens children's eyes to possibilities.

In other words, what will be the "diamond" in Frank's life, or Elizabeth's? For instance, Frank talks about wanting to be first a football player, and then an astronaut. And I tell him, "Well, some day you can play football on the moon." Elizabeth has talked about wanting to be a kindergarten teacher. And what a diamond that could be for the chance to influence young lives for the better.

Richard and I have this expression that we use about the children, "When they see it, they'll know it." "It" can be a terrific diamond, a very good stage play, a wonderful museum. It's important that you teach your children what's quality and what's not. Otherwise, how will they ever know?

Speaking of quality, how about the way you let your children spend their time? Is much of it (apart from homework) invested in watching the tube? I used to be the kind of person that could stay up late, late into the night watching TV. Years ago, Tom Snyder had a show that came on *after* Johnny Carson—in other words, *very* late. I used to watch that show. I was a person who also would sleep in as late as I could.

When I stopped watching television and sleeping late, I found a whole other life.

I found better time with my husband, better time with my children, and time to just relax and do nothing.

Usually these days we go to bed early as a family—at 8:30 or 9 p.m. I have found that there's something about sleeping with the earth that seems to work with me, just as many farm families do. I'm up at 5:30 or 6 a.m. nowadays, and I mean *up!* Awake, ready to roll! No alarm clock wakes me. The sun rises, the shades are open, and when the sun hits me, I'm up! I start the day with the earth.

For me, two hours in the morning are worth five in the evening; I'm that much more productive.

What's more, my children don't have the sense that adults "stay up" much later than children in the evening. They just assume that after dinner, and after the sun has gone down, everyone goes to bed. That again is very bonding. We all go to sleep at the same hour. It's not like the children are being "sent to bed," and the TV's still going in the living room with Mom and Dad up watching the late news. This is extremely good for promoting healthy feelings of "being family." If sleep is out of the question for you at the time you put the children to bed, at least be quiet. Anything that calms the house down in the late evening will be healthy.

Let me tell you a story about a boy who's out looking for his mother. I can't remember exactly where I got it, probably from a book or magazine. Mother and son have been separated in a crowd in some bustling downtown area. The police find the boy and ask him, "What does your mother look like?" and he tells them, "She is the most beautiful, *beautiful* woman I've ever seen; she has long blonde hair and these large green eyes." When, in response to appeals aired on the radio, the woman shows up at the police station to be reunited with her son, she turns out to be an older woman whose beauty has obviously faded. Her hair is not blonde but dark ash turning to gray, and though her eyes are green, they are small and edged with wrinkles. In the eyes of her son, however, she is, quite clearly, a stunning and wonderful woman, inside and out.

That's how I'd like my children to view *me* as I grow older. Isn't this what a mother should hope for?

-» -» -» -» ꙮ «- «- «- «-

After your immediate family, there are obviously other people you love and with whom you want to spend privileged time: extended family (if you can get to them, or they to you), good neighbors, other friends, people with whom you work who have become friends, clients and vendors (who may also, in the best of circumstances, become friends), and people from your church community, your fraternal organization, or other social club.

Extended family tends to be a tough one for many Americans. We have moved around so much, haven't we? Too often there's no aunt coming to visit in the late afternoon. That aunt is either working or she lives someplace else.

The front porches, if people have them at all, often remain empty. The kinds of big neighborhood front-porch gatherings—with uncles, aunts, cousins and the neighbors all piled together—have become, for most of us, distant memories. This is truly a shame.

If there is anything our country desperately needs, it is to recreate a sense of genuine community.

Community means connection, caring, support—just what the doctor would order to combat the high stress and craziness of our rush-about lifestyles.

One way to reconnect is through friends. Sometimes these connections will be through neighbors, like my friend Suzanne, who started by trading child watching with me. I find that I really relate to other women who are doing the high-wire act like I am, trying to blend demanding careers with mothering and homemaking.

These may be author-clients of mine, editors, literary agents, marketing people from companies we represent, or simply people I've met at seminars or other business gatherings. Mostly, they understand the kind of pressures I deal with every day at work. Recently I was talking on the phone to a business associate who has become a good friend, and we got disconnected. We didn't call each other back. We both knew instinctively that the conversation was nearly over, and that each of us had other things to do. Between good friends these unspoken understandings will develop naturally. It's one way you can know when you are truly "in synch" with somebody else.

We give privileged time to our clients every holiday season by baking our favorite cookies and sending them in gaily made-up packages with other homemade goodies. Clients are always amazed by this personal touch. "It's incredible that you would take the time to do something like this for me!" is a typical comment. One client told me last year that waiting for our package to arrive was one of the best things about the season.

So in case you're inspired to start your own tradition of personalizing your gifts to clients and friends, here's a recipe to get you started:

Chocolate-Pecan Angels

1 cup mini semisweet chocolate chips
1 cup chopped pecans, toasted
1 cup sifted powdered sugar
1 egg white

Preheat oven to 350ºF. Grease cookie sheets. Combine chips, pecans and powdered sugar in medium bowl. Add egg white; mix well. Drop batter by teaspoonfuls 2 inches apart onto prepared cookie sheets. Bake 11 to 12 minutes or until edges are light golden brown. Let cookies stand on cookie sheets 1 minute. Remove cookies to wire racks; cool completely.

Makes about 3 dozen cookies

To the greatest extent possible I choose to develop friendships with people who are "alive," who are really *thinking* (not just going through the motions in their jobs or in life), who care about, and consequently take good care of, their minds and bodies.

These are some of the boundaries I have drawn around my family and myself.

Maintaining a quality life sometimes means saying "no." When people are not "right" for the culture we have created at Rocks-DeHart Public Relations, we turn them down as prospective clients. When somebody I have hired proves unable to juggle the multiple tasks that go with our office—put down this, turn your attention to that, then return to the first thing—I have to say, "This isn't working out." And when people try to take up my time whining about their unfortunate lot in life, I have to find ways to minimize any negative effects on me.

I truly believe in synchronicity. When everything is flowing—from home to work and back again—when the talent and the quality are there, everything comes to you. When it flows, it flows right.

My partner, Dottie DeHart, lived in the same townhouse complex I did when I first came to Hickory. She used to stop by and say "hello." Sometimes she would bring a pie. One day she saw me and mentioned that my car was rarely in its parking space.

"Absolutely right," I told her. "I'm working like crazy, day and night."

"Well," she said, "I have a little time between the graduate classes I'm taking. If you ever need any help...."

"I could sure use someone to pick up some envelopes for me at Office Depot," I told her.

Dottie did indeed pick up the envelopes, and now she pretty much runs the company. She has also become one of my closest friends. That's the sort of serendipity that develops when you're living "in the flow."

If you've been paying attention, honey, here is what I hope you got:

- "Quality time" with your family is important. Recognize that it isn't that easy to do, and find creative ways to do it, such as taking your children to their music or dance lessons and staying to watch them.

- Follow your children's progress in school closely and lovingly. Get to know their teachers. If their educational needs are not being met, find a school where they will be.

- "Show up" for important events in your children's lives, such as Little League baseball games.

- Eat together as a family as much as possible—*especially* at home.

- Travel with your children. Show them as much of the world as you can. Contribute to their education on each trip.

- Limit your family's television watching, both the children's and the adults'. A whole new life awaits you once you free yourselves from the magnetic pull of the tube.

- Create genuine community around you to the extent possible. Connect with relatives, neighbors, and friends. You'll find that you will not only offer but also receive caring and support.

- To maintain a quality life, you will have to set boundaries. This means saying "no" to certain activities and certain people. Pay attention to who and what is "in synch" with who you are, and develop your relationships accordingly.

CHAPTER NINE

Develop a Healthy Relationship to $$$

Sylvia, sitting this late afternoon across from my desk, shook back the strawberry blonde hair that had been edging into her eyes, smiled broadly, and said, "I'm glad you like my portfolio of articles and blurbs. I think I can contribute to your services here. So I'm wondering, if you take me on as a freelance writer and editor, could you guarantee me maybe $30,000 a year?"

"Why do you need that sort of guarantee?" I asked her.

"Well, I'm sorry to be that way, but my husband and I have a lot of debt."

I thought to myself, what a tragedy, to live your life as a function of the debt you've gotten yourself into. Then I answered her question:

"Sylvia, that's too bad. I'm so sorry. However, currently we would just prefer to hire the expertise of a freelancer. Could we start working with you on one project at a time, pay you for it, and see how it goes?"

Sylvia went away to ponder her situation, and then did start working on projects for us. However, her debt was always an

95

issue, and ended up suffocating her so that she stopped free-lancing and went to look for a full-time job. Sylvia was unable to take intelligent risks because her debt served as a ball and chain.

Working to pay off debt is a hard place to be. I know because I have "been there, done that." Nonetheless, it is a crucible of suffering that you absolutely must put yourself through if indeed your debt load is "off the charts," because until and unless you do, you cannot get on with living the good life that you have been dreaming about. The good life means, among other things, being as debt free as possible (though mortgages and car payments can be OK).

If there is any way you can commit yourself to getting completely out of debt, I would tell you that there is probably no other activity that you could undertake that would be as valuable. That's because a debt load absolutely influences every other aspect of your life—the time you have for relationships, the way you approach intelligent risk in business, how much of the world you are able to see, and the day-to-day stress you experience.

People who are crippled by debt actually reflect that condition in their emotional bearing. They experience being in shackles—to banks, department stores, credit-card companies, or whomever. And it doesn't feel good living your life in shackles.

I checked my e-mail and there I found yet another credit-card offer.

"Too many credit cards in this world already," I comment-ed to Megan. "What we need is not a better credit card, but fewer of them—or maybe none at all. We're under incredible pressure to spend, spend, and SPEND—all the time. Every time you walk into a department store, they're offering you a card. The banks, too. And direct mail and advertising in the media. I don't think most people even understand how much pressure they're under to keep putting things on plastic."

"That bad, Ceil?" Megan asked as she joined my conversa-tion.

"Probably worse," I said. "Credit-card debt is the bane of our society. Oh, I think we have to keep one card—just for travel, etc., because the hotels all want you to pay that way, but you have to be very, very disciplined. And if you can't, you have to get radical with yourself."

"How radical?" Megan ventured.

"Cut those cards up and throw them away. Use only a debit card, where you have to have the money in the bank or the card won't be accepted. Or better still, just carry cash."

"CASH!?!" Megan almost shouted.

"Yes, cash," I insisted.

"Forget plastic, sharply cut back on your use of checks. Pay in cash. This is especially true for people who have gotten themselves into trouble with running up credit-card tabs they cannot manage, or who have not kept good track of their checkbook and have started committing overdrafts. These peo-ple need radical surgery in their financial habits.

"You get yourself some little white envelopes and write on each one what the money is for. Let's say you put $500 in one for groceries and eating out for the month. You put $100 in another, and that's for your car expenses. Another envelope is for other purchases—sundries, inexpensive clothing items, and so forth. Of course, you probably still have to pay your mortgage or your rent with a check, but I would suggest that you pay those bills through direct banking, whenever possible."

"That sounds like a whole lot of trouble, paying so much in cash," Megan said in her most skeptical tone of voice.

"It doesn't have to be forever, just until a person acquires some solid financial discipline. It really does reinforce for you what you're spending when you see the money leaving your hands in cash, believe me. In most cases, people take stock, and if they've been living on the moon about their financial habits, they start to come down to earth and make changes."

"I tried it for a while, just to experience what Ceil was talking about," Dottie said to Megan. "I mean, I wasn't really very undisciplined myself, but I wanted to get that feel of kissing my cash good-bye. It works. *All* of my spending became much more *conscious* as a result of using cash so much."

"I'll give it a whirl," Megan decided. "Just to see."

The weather outside was turning gray and stormy, I noticed. Whereas the sun had been glimmering faintly over the morning haze when I drove to work, now clouds were massing on the horizon, and I thought I perceived flickers of lightning in the distance.

"Do you hear any thunder?" I asked my two associates.

"I do," Charity, our intern said. "Way off."

"Dottie," I said, "would you turn on the radio? Maybe they'll announce something about the storm."

Dottie did and after a few minutes an announcer broke into the music with a bulletin:

"The weather bureau has issued a severe thunderstorm warning, with possible tornadoes forming and a chance of flash floods in rivers and creeks. You are advised to shut down all electronic equipment, stay off the telephone unless it's an emergency, and keep tuned to this station for updates on storm conditions."

"You'd better get going, both of you, before you get caught in really bad weather," I told them. "I think I'll shut things down here and run by the kids' school and see if they will let parents take their children home early. We have a nice secure family room downstairs, and that's where I'd like us to be in case there are torrential downpours."

"Right, Ceil. Thanks for thinking about all of us."

"Go," I said. "Let's move on out of here."

Driving to Frank and Elizabeth's school through the first wave of sporadic rainfall, I reflected on how storms and storm warnings can be understood as metaphors for our financial behavior and the consequences that ensue. What everybody needs is a good storm cellar to ride things out, like our family room. You don't want to be caught short, with no provisions, no safe place to hunker down, in case things turn stormy for your finances—someone in the family loses an important job, or serious injury or sickness strikes, and suddenly you're left facing major medical bills or any number of things that could be compared to a lightning bolt or a cyclone wreaking havoc.

Richard and I have spent considerable time and energy discussing readiness to meet sudden trouble to protect our family from the ravages of a financial thunderstorm.

Some of these things may work for you, and some may seem too "far out." I'm going to go through a short list of preparedness tactics anyway. I do hope you'll choose at least one or two and try them out.

-》 -》 -》 -》 ⚘ 《- 《- 《- 《-

- Pay ahead on your mortgage. It is fairly commonplace financial advice to pay at least one extra installment a year on your mortgage, with the overage going entirely to principal. That builds up equity and can in the end let you pay off your mortgage five to seven years ahead of schedule, saving you tens of thousands of dollars. And I recommend that. But what I'm talking about here is actually having three or more *monthly payments* into the bank *ahead of their due* dates. This way, if anything happens to your family, you can be worry free about your mortgage payments for at least that time, while you marshal your assets, redo loans, or whatever else it takes to restore balance to your financial ship. I think the process gives you emotional breathing room.

- Pay ahead on your utility bills. Same principle as above. The gas, water, and electric companies in your area will be happy to accept money beyond your current bills due, and hold it against future payments. Then just keep paying your monthly bills as usual. If anything untoward strikes your family, you'll have your utilities secured for those three or more months, just like your mortgage.

- Keep an emergency fund on hand. This should be a separate bank account—or it could double as a vacation account if you're willing to sacrifice a vacation when trouble hits and use the money for necessities. Every individual or family will have to decide what amount would be best, but I would recommend a minimum of $2,000 for an individual, $4,000 for a couple, and an extra $500 or so for each child.

- Store some food and water at home. I know, I know! This makes me sound like a member of one of those survivalist groups. I'm not, trust me. You simply never know, however, what events may occur, from a blackout because of a power-grid failure, to an ice storm, or heaven knows what will cause you to stay at home and ride something out. Three days' supplies may be enough—or you may want more. It's up to you to decide, but do have some provisions on hand against the day when something totally unpredictable occurs in your vicinity.

- Keep your credit good with everybody. Whomever you owe, pay on time—or ahead of time, if at all possible—banks, insurance companies, stores, suppliers, and so on. That way if you ever have an emergency, these people will quite likely remember, or be able to verify, your history of prompt payments, and be able to be generous in extending you credit, because you have not abused their trust in normal circumstances.

Arriving home with my children, I found Richard pulling into the driveway just ahead of me. Great minds think alike. The storm, meanwhile, was continuing with some fury, high winds whipping through the neighborhood and setting trees into a blustery dance of perilous dips and sways.

"Whew! Some storm, huh, Ceil?" Richard called to me above the whistling of the wind and the staccato beat of the rain. We were already standing in the garage, having parked our cars side by side. Frank and Elizabeth had already fled into the house. Silently, Richard and I eyed the automatic garage door, and I knew we were both hoping the same thing: that the door would indeed go down before any power outage occurred. It did—but just barely.

No sooner had we gained the relative safety of our kitchen than the lights fluttered and faded, then extinguished entirely.

"Mommeee!!!" Elizabeth's voice reached us from her bedroom.

Frank appeared a moment later, candles in hand and ready to pitch in with whatever.

"You're on it!" Richard exclaimed, gleeful.

"Look," I said, "Let's just stay calm and have a good time as a family, shall we?

"Frank, why don't you light some candles in the family room and get yourself and Elizabeth down there. Bring your sleeping bags, too. We may all just camp out tonight. Your Dad and I can open up the queen-sized sofa bed, and we'll just be snug and cozy. I think we'll get cold cuts from the fridge and plan to eat down there, too; how would that be?"

"Nice idea, Mom," Frank replied.

"Mommee, can we watch television down there?" Elizabeth asked. She was clearly over her initial fright.

"Why don't we just plan to talk and play board games, honey," I said. "Anyway, the power is off, and the TV won't work. You should also know, however, that TVs can be dangerous in a storm."

"This house could weather any storm, especially with an ounce of prevention," Richard commented.

"That's the way we want it, isn't it?" I said.

The children chimed, "You bet."

We have had a lot of happy times in our homes because they are never a financial burden for us. At that point we were trying to pay off our mortgage instead of finding more things to buy and stuff in it. It was another financial goal Richard and I had set for ourselves, though in truth, that kind of thinking originated with him, not me. I have now fully bought into it, but it took some help from a client to nudge me over toward Richard's perspective.

I asked several clients of best-selling books on personal finance, "What's best—should I pay down my mortgage, or shall I keep paying on it and use it every year as a write-off on income taxes? And then put the money I would have used on extra mortgage payments into mutual funds?"

Here's the gist of what these clients said to me: "Why don't you pay down your mortgage because of the emotional value to you of doing that? Money should work to make you feel comfortable."

I reminded Richard that some clients had to chip in their two cents' worth before I would agree to paying down the mortgage.

"I'm always happy to have help getting my opinions across to you," Richard laughed. "But what kind of a feeling do you get knowing we're working toward a goal that spells freedom?"

"It's a really great feeling," I said. "Just think: Month after month will come by, and there will be no mortgage payment due at the bank. Zero! *Niente!* How wonderful!"

We were now all ensconced in the family room, with eight candles glowing on the mantle, end tables, and other strategic places. There was enough light to see our cold cuts and chips and move the tokens on the board games, and though lightning was flashing, thunder roaring, and rains pounding on the pane glass, we felt safe and snug as a family.

"Spend on doing, especially education, rather than having," Richard remarked, as he and I carried on with some family finance notes even as we played a game with Frank and Elizabeth.

"You mean like going to New York!" Frank piped up.

"Exactly!" I replied. "And to Europe, too."

"You mean like learning to play the violin!" Elizabeth said.

"Good!" said her father.

And do you know—that's precisely what our family does. Our furniture is all bought. It is good quality stuff; it will wear well; and I have no desire to change it, or add to it. Furniture buying is done. We're focused on paying off our mortgage. We have ample savings in the bank and now also in some other investments. What we are now free to do is invest in the children's education, both formal and informal—such as family trips to broaden their view of the world.

In my mind I was saying to myself that Richard's last remark was the perfect way to close out this chapter, but he had one more maxim to remind us about:

"Use what you have—use it up, and then replace it."

"Like soap, Dad?" Frank wanted to know.

"Right—just like soap. Clothes, sheets, towels, toys… whatever. Have just what you need—have the right kind of things—and then nothing goes onto the high shelf in a closet; it all gets worn, used, until it needs replacing."

"Like lipstick, Mommy?" Elizabeth chimed in.

"Right again," I spoke up. "I know lots of ladies who keep buying, buying, buying lipsticks like there's no tomorrow, and before you know it, they have seventeen different shades. Well, guess what usually happens: they wear only three or four of those shades. The other lipsticks just sit there gathering dust. That's what Daddy's saying we shouldn't be doing."

"Hey, while you guys were talking, I just won the game!" Frank announced.

And so he had. We slept soundly as the storm raged outside. And in my dreams that night, Richard and I were boarding a plane for Geneva to show Frank and Elizabeth a beautiful part of the world.

If you've been paying attention, honey, here is what I hope you got:

- Make paying off debt the first objective of your financial plan. And put credit-card debt first.

- Stop biting on credit-card offers. If at all possible, reduce your cards to just one, just for the absolute necessities.

- If you have been financially irresponsible with credit cards, cut up ALL your cards so that you won't be tempted to use them again. Use only a debit card, where you have to have money in the bank for the card to be accepted.

- More radical still, pay everything you can in cash. At the beginning of each month, put cash in envelopes earmarked "groceries," "gas," "sundries," etc. Experience the feeling of money leaving your possession when you pay in cash. It will make you *much more conscious of how you are spending*.

- Bear down on financial preparedness for the unexpected. Pay ahead on your mortgage and your utility bills, and keep an emergency fund on hand.

- Keep your credit good with everybody: pay on time or ahead of time. Then if you ever need a credit extension due to something unexpected, banks, and stores are all likely to be generous.

- Make it a goal to pay off your mortgage as early as possible. There is nothing like the feeling of financial independence you get when you own your home 100 percent. Owning your home completely represents a terrific investment. That freedom is more valuable than any tax deduction you could get. And of course, it's easier to pay off a smaller home than one that keeps choking you to make large payments, month after month, year after year.

- Spend on doing rather than on having. Rather than buying more objects to take up room in your house, invest in educational and cultural opportunities, family outings, and travel. These kinds of investments will remain a part of you—and your children—and will last a lifetime.

- Use whatever you possess—use it up, and then replace it. Let nothing gather dust on a shelf or in a drawer or, worse, boxed up in storage in your attic. "Use it up, wear it out, make it do, or do without," as my college roommate's father used to say.

CHAPTER TEN

Work Hard and Play Hard

"Mmmm, this sun does feel good," Suzanne confessed as she flipped from her back onto her tummy, and stretched out again on the chaise longue at the community pool. "I'm still feeling guilty taking time away from the pharmacy in mid-afternoon, but I'm counting on your experience and instincts, Ceil, that this'll be good for me."

I looked up from my yellow legal pad full of whimsical doodling and spoke to her back as she lay glistening with tanning oil. "Don't worry; it's good. With more practice you'll be able to do it without the guilt."

Frank and Elizabeth were playing tag in the water with Suzanne's two children, Joy and Bobby. We had hired Nickie, my runner (not my usual babysitter), to watch the four of them. That way I could get some creative work done.

"Don't let me bother you, Ceil," Suzanne murmured.

"Not to worry. You sound as if you're almost asleep. I'll try to watch that you don't bake your back too deeply—just relax and enjoy."

In serendipity fashion, while my children frolicked and my friend Suzanne dozed, a host of fresh ideas for promoting my latest client were taking shape on the legal pad. It took getting out of the office and into the fresh air to make it happen.

Where did we ever get the notion that to be "really working" you have to be glued to an office chair, sitting at a desk, and working with a sheaf of papers and, in case you needed some research material, a metal file cabinet close at hand? A friend once suggested that the origin of "working at your desk" was the old ink pen, the kind that had to be dipped into an inkwell. You weren't going to go carrying an inkwell around with you so that you could put down a thought. That meant you had to stay near your desk in order to write. We're in a different world today, what with cell phones, laptops, and other high-tech goodies—and there's absolutely no good reason to stay strapped to a desk all the time.

I was with my uncle recently, and he had his car phone on voice activation. He spoke out, "Phone, call home!" and the phone dialed his home number. That's a long way from the inkwell!

What I was doing poolside was productive daydreaming. Time off, but with an eye to generating, or crystalizing, some ideas. I don't think, in truth, that my best work has ever been done sitting at a desk. My best work can happen while I'm driving down the street. Or taking a walk.

People will say things about work like, "You have to be realistic." What they mean is "keep your nose to the grindstone," or "tough it out." In other words, work is not meant to be much fun. Working "hard" for these types means "suffer through it."

But I disagree.

I remember when I was struggling in television as an assistant to the producer of a morning show. The producer would take his whole staff, including me, to the nicest hotel he could find in Miami, and he'd rent the best suite. Then he would order for all of us the most scrumptious food on the menu. And all day long we would sit in this beautiful suite overlooking the ocean and brainstorm ideas for the show.

Was that producer being extravagant or wasteful? Not at all. The brainstorming that took place in that relaxing setting led to some terrific ideas for the show—ideas that translated into the show doing well and making good money for the station.

It's OK, however, to go on a "work binge" every now and then—especially when you feel you are really "in the groove."

My husband travels a lot in his business, and sometimes he takes the children out of town with him. On those occasions, I've been known to turn in a frenzied weekend of work. I may go into my office at 6 a.m. on a Friday morning and work straight through the weekend—I'm talking about working three straight twelve-hour days, with time out for lunch each day to gather my thoughts.

At such times I feel the energy moving me along. I feel "in synch." And I can get a lot accomplished.

At other times, though, I know that I'm just not being productive, and I need some downtime. Then I simply have to leave the office. I may go anywhere. I happen to like stationery shops, so I may browse in one. I enjoy choosing different kinds of paper and pens for our office and for my personal use, so that's a fun thing for me. Or I may go to a bookstore and mosey around, or check out some books from the library. *I will not work when I'm not ready to work!* When I am ready, nobody can work harder than I can—just watch out!

Being at the pool this day was the best of both worlds: a relaxing experience that also resulted in a raft of new ideas for promoting a client. After two hours of splashing, Suzanne's and my children were ready to dry off and go home. Suzanne had to get back to the pharmacy, and I was ready to sit down at my Mac and put some meat on the skeleton of the marketing program I had sketched.

This was one of those win-win-wins we all love to have.

-»› -»› -»› -»› ✽ «‹- «‹- «‹- «‹-

"There's nothing that can be more aggravating than the wrong clients, right, Ceil?" Leslie remarked during our staff meeting later.

"Right on. It's really a matter of matching cultures."

"Matching cultures? Sounds like microbiology."

"I mean workplace cultures—values, expectations, attitudes, even ways of doing things."

"Can you give me an example?"

"Yes, Leslie, I think I can. Once, you may recall, I was helping a local advertising agency with an account of theirs. They had me come to a meeting with them, and suddenly I found myself in the middle of a good-old boys' club.

"I presented my part of the project, and gave it quite a boost, and I thought I had done pretty well. But a few days later, my associate from the advertising agency, who had invited me to the meeting, called me over.

"I said to him, 'Well, did they like my presentation?'

"'They said you were a little bit aggressive,' he replied.

"'Gee, Charlie,' I said, 'I wasn't *aggressive*. I was just trying to get it done because I thought that meeting was moving rather slowly.'"

I felt badly for a few days, and then, by happenstance, I was talking on the phone to Dr. Henrie Weisinger, author of *Emotional Intelligence at Work*. He's one of the premier experts in the country on emotional intelligence. So I took the opportunity to run by him what had happened to me at the advertising planning meeting.

"'Dr. Weisinger,' I said, 'I was just devastated by their response to my presentation. I just worked a project and did my job; I don't think I was too aggressive.'

"I'll never forget what he said to me:

"*If they said you were too aggressive, Celia, then you were too aggressive. How people perceive you is how you are, whether you agree with that perception or not.*'

"And he counseled me about 'matching cultures.' In other words, an emotionally intelligent person has to analyze a scene carefully before behaving one way or another. You have to match up to the people with whom you are working. This is usually understood to mean "dress like they do," but in actuality, it goes much further than that."

"Whew!" Leslie said. "I hadn't heard that story from you before. You hadn't let on to us what happened with that advertising agency thing. That is *quite* a challenge—matching cultures. And I guess you have to do it all without coming on as some artificial distortion of your real self, huh?"

"I would say so. But don't expect me to get into any of the fine points on this. This is something I'm just beginning to learn myself."

Sometimes working hard is simply a matter of creativity. What's the point of staying at the office for nine hours straight beating your brains out if what you really need is a creative breakthrough—something that might happen in two minutes if you maybe just took a walk in the park and thought things through?

We like to say around my office, "Failure is not an option." Just like the line in the movie "Apollo 13" when Mission Control was determined to get the astronauts back from outer space after a major systems breakdown.

One day a prospective client walked into our office carrying the book he had just published. He was a wonderful man, a man who definitely "gets the picture," a man highly successful in his field, which involved coaching companies on management techniques, and training. The cover of his book, however, was awful.

"This is the worst book cover I've ever seen," I had to tell him candidly. "Don't worry, though. We're going to work the problem."

"How?" he said, afraid to be too hopeful after my comment about the cover.

"Do you know what?" I responded quickly as a burst of creativity swept over me. "We're just not going to show your book cover to anybody in the media until *after* we've already sold them on the value of your material. We won't put the book jacket, or even a picture of it, in the press kit. Because I *don't* want them to judge a book by its cover!"

"Hmmm," he said. "Whatever you say. I hope it works."

It did. We highlighted that client's great material, and got him on *ABC World News* and in a host of other spots in national and regional media.

Typically, we work with clients who come to appreciate us—sometimes they even say they love us. This is especially true if we have been successful at matching cultures.

People who "get it," who really want results, can afford us as well; and one of my strategies for my company has been to price ourselves at a level where we can really service our clients well. Our clients are usually very positive; "no whiners allowed." And even though they are paying us, they contribute to the process and give us some good ideas on how we can best promote their books or other products.

Being "in synch" with clients helps make our working days satisfying—even fun.

-» -» -» -» ❧ «- «- «- «-

When I end a workday, however, I like to end it. No dragging work home or habitually working on weekends, or getting up in the middle of the night and racing downstairs to finish a report. That kind of addiction to work will eventually make you sick, and quite possibly break up your family. So what good will all your "hard work" be then?

At home I love to read sitting out on our sun porch or even out on the patio. And I can have all kinds of fun with movies rented from Blockbuster. What's more, I've learned to enjoy my time with people I love as much as anything else in life.

Twice a week, every Tuesday and Thursday morning from 8:00 to 9:00, I work with my personal trainer at the gym. When I first started working with a trainer, I would cancel a lot. "Something's come up at the office," I would tell him. "I can't make it today." Lately, I've stopped letting work get in the way of my time with the trainer. I feel so much better after my workout that I'm sure that my time at the gym is well spent; it simply makes me much more fit to do a great job once I'm back at my Mac or on the phone.

If you get the mix of work, play, rest, and family time right, you'll find that you have achieved much of what "the good life" is about. ❧ ❧ ❧

If you've been paying attention, honey, here is what I hope you got:

- When possible, combine work and pleasure. Sometimes you can be at your most creative in a setting *away from the office.*

- "Working hard" does not have to mean "suffering through it." Find ways to treat yourself to a nice atmosphere when you have something very challenging to accomplish (if at all possible).

- It's OK to go on a "work binge" once in awhile—when you are really "on" … if you are really in the mood for work and you have the energy to get a lot done. Just don't make it a regular habit to "binge."

- When you find that your productivity is low, it's a sign that you need some downtime. If possible, leave your workplace and go browsing in a bookstore, or occupy yourself for at least a short while with something else you like to do.

- Nonetheless, on the whole, demand a high level of achievement from yourself—and from others who work under your supervision or with you as associates or suppliers.

- Learn to "match cultures." Prefer working with people whose values and attitudes are "in synch" with your own. This might begin with a "dress code," but in actuality it goes much further—into ways of presenting yourself and ways of interacting in a group. Being "in synch" with others will make work more satisfying—even fun.

- Adopt a "failure is not an option" mentality. Use creativity and teamwork to brainstorm and innovate your way through to the solutions of whatever problems you encounter.

- When it's time to stop working, STOP!!! Refrain from dragging work into your family time, into your weekends (with *occasional* exceptions), and into your vacations away from home.

- Treat your body to regular workouts, and do not cheat yourself out of the hobbies, sports, and other forms of entertainment that you truly enjoy.

CHAPTER ELEVEN

Dig In and Enjoy where You Are—Or Move!

"Celia, I'm moving—but I don't know exactly where." My editor friend Laura's voice sounded strangely unsteady on the phone connection from San Francisco Bay.

"How unusual!" I replied. "Tell me more."

"Well, I met a wonderful guy a year ago while I was at a convention in Chicago, but he's not from Chicago—he's working with a high-tech company based in the D.C. suburbs... Arlington, to be precise."

"So...you're moving to Virginia?"

"That's a possibility. We're now engaged to get married, and this love of my life—Peter Marvel—isn't that a super name?— has some choices as to where he could be transferred."

"Oh, the mystery unravels; *you* get to help him choose where to be sent?"

"Right. And, oh, Celia...I'm just so baffled about the whole process. I mean this is going to be my *life*."

"I take it that San Francisco is *not* one of his choices?"

"Right again. They're all on the East Coast or in the Southwest."

"How do you feel about leaving San Francisco?"

"That's OK. I'm originally from Delaware and, to tell the truth, I'm not sure I've ever become a 'West Coast Person.' Do you have any idea how I should choose? I'm very familiar with one of the places Peter could be sent—Philadelphia, Pennsylvania—but I don't know much about the other two—Atlanta, Georgia, or Abilene, Texas. I guess he could also stay where he is, in Arlington."

"Where is Peter from originally?"

"Actually, he was born and raised in the D.C. suburbs, although he went to school in Indiana and then in Pennsylvania, and had duty in the Air Force in Florida."

"So he's an 'East Coast Person' like you?"

"Yes, I'd say so."

"Good. That makes it much easier. That would be my first 'cut.' Are you 'East Coast' or 'West Coast' or 'Midwest' or something like that. How do you do with very hot weather, Laura?"

"Not too well, actually. And I think that Peter suffered a bit, too, when he was stationed in Panama City with the Air Force."

"OK. So perhaps you may want to think twice about Abilene, Texas—and maybe Atlanta as well."

"Hmmm. I see what you mean."

"And then it sounds as if you both might have family in that area between Philadelphia and D.C.?"

"Yes, we do, in fact. Mine are scattered around the area

between Newark, Delaware, and New York state, and Peter's family is pretty much in Virginia."

"Family is important, Laura. You are blessed if you can be near your family."

"Do you know what? I think one reason I've been unhappy here in San Francisco is that it's just too far away from the people I care about: my parents, my younger brother, and quite a few uncles and aunts, nieces and nephews. I also miss the people I was close to in college, the University of Maryland. Most of them are still in the East."

"Maybe it's a flip of the coin between Philadelphia and Arlington then," I suggested.

"Hey, that sounds right! And at this point, I think I'd be just as happy tossing it back into Peter's lap. I'd rather he make the final choice based on what would work best for him job-wise."

"Good idea. Hope it works out for both of you—and don't forget to invite me to the wedding!"

After Laura and I said "Sayonara," I sat at my desk musing about location.

It has, I reflected, *enormous* influence on one's life. Where you live and work, and what's around you day by day—your environment—can be the difference between sleeping well with pleasant dreams, or tossing and turning through a nightmare of being chained to a railroad track with a freight train emerging from the tunnel and headed your way.

That's why I like to counsel friends to do one of two things: either make your peace with where you are, and throw your energies into making it as nice an experience as possible—or else get on a research track to find another place to live.

The secret of location is that everything's a tradeoff. In moving away from South Florida, where I had grown up, I gave up proximity to the Atlantic Ocean and those gorgeous beaches. Along the way I exchanged it for a wonderful four-season climate, hills and proximity to mountains, a sense of community, a beautiful bucolic neighborhood, and practically zero crime rate.

Nonetheless, after a number of very pleasant and rewarding years in Hickory, North Carolina, Richard and I decided to establish another base for our life—in the Pittsburgh area. That is where Richard is from and where we have an abundance of wonderful family and friends. We maintained our home in Hickory for a time and came to feel that we were able to enjoy the best of both worlds. Being a joyful simplifier doesn't mean you have to limit your choices to the bare bones; it means that you can have *more* of the things that work for you and make your life fulfilling. It also means that you'll know how to simplify no matter where you go, and thus you'll enjoy many options.

Here's what I say: If where you are currently is not where you feel good living, have no fear of moving. Life is an adventure. There's a whole wide world out there waiting for you.

On the other hand, of course, be sure you have counted the blessings of the place where you are now. It may be more what you need than you think—especially if your location keeps you in touch with family and friends that you cherish. I would caution you against being too hasty in giving up proximity to people you love and whose friendship you count upon.

In the case of Richard and me, we were fortunate to be in businesses that allowed us to move with relative ease. I wasn't planted in Hickory—I researched it and sought it out. When I was satisfied it could give me and my family the kind of life we wanted, I chose it. Then, when it made sense for us to be closer to family and friends in Pittsburgh, we moved there.

Do a checklist for yourself. You might begin by eliminating the sorts of place you *don't* want to be:

What's important for *you*?

- Big city living—major museums, theatres, professional sports, upscale shopping.
- Small city living—lower cost of living, lower crime rate, less traffic, but still with cultural amenities such as community theatre, concerts, etc.
- Small town or rural living—peace and quiet, closeness to nature.
- Proximity to the ocean (or lake).
- Proximity to mountains (or hills).
- Tropical climate.
- Four-season climate.
- Quality schools (if you have children).
- Opportunities for taking courses in higher education.
- Numerous job opportunities.
- Good neighbors.

- _____
- _____
- _____
- _____
- _____

You will no doubt have your own "bullet points" to add to the list. After you have added these, go down the list and make checks (or double checks if the item is super important to you). Notice also where you did *not* make a check. This checklist will serve as the start of your search if you are intent on changing your location.

→» →» →» →» ⚘ «– «– «– «–

Distance from home to work can be an issue. I know of a married woman who lives in a large metropolitan area and who has to commute one and a half hours each way to work—*daily.* She recently told me she's decided not to have a baby because she just wouldn't have the time with her job and that three-hour commute. How *awful!* I mean, it would be one thing if she truly did not want children for other reasons, but to forego having a child just because you have too much of a commute! That's not a very good reason. In her case, she should look at changing jobs, or moving, or some type of flexible commuting schedule if it would mean she could go ahead and have a child.

And I say that as a woman who has been extremely fulfilled by being able to be both a mother and a business owner.

That's one of the nicer things that my life in Hickory allowed: I had my office in a commercial building just two miles from my house. I could literally cut short a phone conversation at the office and tell the other party, "I'll call you back in ten minutes from home," and do it. I learned from that experience how to duplicate that arrangement in a larger city. Now in Pittsburgh, I have an office in a small commercial building with a view of the river in a bucolic setting. I live just ten minutes from the office in an area seven miles north of downtown, and I go against the general traffic flow as I drive to and from work.

If indeed you are contemplating a move, I highly recommend *visiting* your new intended location as frequently as you can over a period of months before you take the plunge. Use your vacation time, long holiday weekends, whatever you can—just *go there and experience the place.* That gives you a chance to see many neighborhoods and also explore the surrounding area.

The other thing I'd say is *rent first*—do *not* buy a home immediately.

Renting helps you meet people—in your apartment building or apartment complex. You can then take your time and go to open houses on Sundays and have a realtor show you the range of condos or houses on the market. Never rush a home purchase. *You are much less likely to make a mistake in your home purchase if you start out from a rented dwelling and take time to explore the new area.*

"Oh, Ceil, I like that flower arrangement you got for yourself this week!" It was Leslie, stopping by my door to say "hi" before she took off to visit a client of ours in Atlanta.

"Thanks, Leslie. I hope you're doing something nice for your work area at home, too."

"Not as regularly as you, I'm afraid. Once in a while I get myself some flowers—but not every week like you do."

"Well, it's *your* space. Treat yourself like a queen, and other people will too. I'm not saying this for you, because I know you have your work space set up pretty nicely, but it amazes me how many people just don't put any energy at all into decorating the place where they work. Some of them say, 'It's not my property after all; I'm not going to spend money adding to what my employer has done for the space.' That's so short-sighted! If you feel that way you are only cheating yourself. You may as well make your space just as pleasant as possible for yourself, even if it means leaving some of your decorating to the next occupant of the space if you move on."

"That does make a lot of sense, doesn't it?" Leslie finished.

"Yes, it does. I say, bring nice things to work—*surround* yourself with nice things—artwork, photos, mementos. You'll be much happier at work, and probably will do a better job because of being in a good mood."

As Leslie departed, I thought of our different preferences.

Leslie enjoys working from her home and has a completely equipped, and tastefully furnished, home office. I do not do well working from home. I like a complete separation between home life and office life, and enjoy being in rented space in a commercial building in Pittsburgh.

This is an issue each person has to sort out for himself or herself. I can't do it for you. I thought I would, however, list some of the pros and cons of working from home. This list might help you decide.

Working from home can be good because:
- You eliminate your commute entirely.
- You have more time available to work.
- You can alternate your professional work with some gardening or routine household chores—or even take a shower or give yourself an exercise or meditation break. Some people can be quite productive that way.
- Unless you expect business visitors, you can dress as casually as you like.
- You avoid the expenses of renting an office.
- And (best of all, according to some) you can deduct a portion of your house from your taxes as a legitimate business expense—and also deduct pro rata shares of your utilities.

Working from home can be a negative because:
- It is hard to truly separate your work life from your home life.

- Children and other family members, and their demands, can interfere with your work.
- Business visitors may be uncomfortable meeting with you at your home. (For instance, the bathroom can be an issue. You don't want an early morning visitor using a bathroom where the steam from your shower is still evident on the glass sliding door to the tub.)
- Too many things around the house may prove an unproductive distraction—television, unmade beds, laundry waiting to be done, or neighbors dropping over.
- Employees (when you grow into needing them) may not want to report to your home to work for you.
- Some of your clients or customers may consider you "too small" if they perceive that you are working from home instead of from a commercial building. (This will vary greatly according to your field.)
- Commercial rent is, of course, deductible.

As a postscript to this chapter, I'd like to say a word to you about the value of friendships as an important part of your life arena. Perhaps we put too much emphasis on physical surroundings, and not nearly enough on the *people* we try to bring into the spaces in our lives. People are much more important than furniture or wall hangings or whether we look out upon a park or a pond.

One of the main reasons we Americans can never be satisfied is that we're too focused on pursuing money, possessions, and financial security. We don't spend nearly enough energy pursuing friendship—or community.

People who have wonderful friends—friends they enjoy being with, friends they can count on—have a great life. Developing good, solid friendships is also a way to build community. And the good times you'll get out of having good friends is something that money can't buy.

The old saying, "To make a friend, be a friend," is as true today as it ever was. You cannot simply wait for somebody to show up on your doorstep and ask to be your friend. You've got to look around and see who you'd enjoy spending time with, and, quite literally, *pursue* that friendship.

I believe we hold back from pursuing friendships because we are afraid of rejection. If you make an overture to someone, and he or she does not respond, then you tend to feel hurt. This is natural, but I think we just have to take that risk if we ever want to turn acquaintances into friends.

When I lived in Miami I had a woman pursue friendship with me. She would come to my office, invite me out to lunch, do whatever she could to be my friend. If I said I couldn't make lunch, she'd say, "Well, next time." Then she would invite me out again.

This is a married woman who was part of a major law practice, and had a very busy life. Yet she valued deep friendship and somehow decided I was worth her efforts. Because of her energy in pursuing friendship, we did indeed become close friends. I am a better person because she decided she wanted me to be part of her life and was willing to do the work. We are all so busy trying to have it all that sometimes we forget to put the work into new friendships.

Our high-tech world has insulated us from the human contacts that were part of American life in the 50s and 60s. The minute we started depending on our cell phones and spending time on our home computers surfing the net, we got off our porches—or stopped building porches. We escaped into our own little worlds where we did not know any longer who our neighbors were. I believe we need to recapture some of our past ways of dealing with people *personally*—of saying "hi" to the mail carrier and actually knowing his or her name, of taking a moment to exchange a story or at least a smile with the people we meet every day.

When you find the "perfect" place to live, make it even more perfect by helping to build community.

If you've been paying attention, honey, here is what I hope you got:

- Your physical location is an important part of the good life. First, count your blessings in the place where you are—especially if those blessings include closeness to family or friends. Do not give up too hastily on where you are currently located.

- However, after due consideration, you may actually decide you have to be in a place that's better for you. If you do decide to move, determine what general area of the country you feel best in—such as the Southeast, Mid-Atlantic, Midwest, Pacific Northwest, etc. Some of you may only need to move to a new part of town!

- Recognize that the secret of location is that everything is a tradeoff. No place will be without its imperfections. Perfection in location is for another life—not the one we have now on the earth.

- Do a checklist for yourself of what's important for you in a location, and what's not. (See pages 123 and 124.)

- If too long a commute is an issue, seriously consider moving—or changing jobs.

- Before you move to another location, visit that area as often as possible and get the feel of the various neighborhoods and what the city or town has to offer.

- When you do move, *rent first.* You will thus take a major step toward avoiding a serious mistake in the purchase of a home that may turn out to be wrong for you.

- Recognize that the space where you work every day is an important influence on your life and your moods. Make that space as pleasant for yourself as possible.

- Whether to work from home or from an office is an important decision. You might start by going through the checklist in this chapter (See pages 127 and 128).

- Friendships are important for the quality of your day-to-day life. Make a commitment to pursue friendship with people in your area whom you consider likely prospects. Move through your fear of rejection, and *do it!*

- Commit yourself to building community with people around you, wherever you decide to live. Get to know your neighbors, the mail carrier, the shopkeepers, and others who supply the products you buy and use. Break through the impersonality of our high-tech society, and restore "the best of the past."

CHAPTER TWELVE

Slow Down, Play, and Take Care of Your Emotional Health

"Life's a banquet—and most poor souls are starving to death," I murmured as I spread mayonnaise on my turkey and Swiss sandwich.

"Ceil! Where did THAT come from?" Richard said, smiling broadly. "Are you taking over as the family's resident philosopher? On second thought, isn't that a quote from *Mame*?"

We were ensconced on a large blanket in a lovely park in Pittsburgh, picnicking on a glorious late summer's day. Frank and Elizabeth, not yet responding to the call to "Come and eat lunch!" were off by a pond feeding bread to the ducks.

"I don't know who the author of that one is, but I can tell you another one I remember that's pretty similar," I said. "'*Most men lead lives of quiet desperation.*' That, I know for sure, is Thoreau."

"I'm impressed," my husband said.

There we were, all together as a family, doing what families are supposed to do on weekends—getting out and enjoying the fresh air, talking about life, and laughing over the antics of the local duck population.

Just then a troupe of girls in their mid-teens swung by, all decked out in prom-style dresses. They must have been on their way to a special gala or dance. A photographer was snapping pictures of them as they skipped along a path in the park.

"Look, Mommie! It's beauty queens!" Elizabeth squealed as she arrived at the blanket for her sandwich.

"Aw, no it isn't," said Frank. "I'll bet they're shooting pictures for a magazine story or an ad." Ah, my son—ever the realist.

"Who knows?" I interjected. "But do you know what? I was once part of doing a show on beauty queens."

"Really, Mom?" my children chorused.

"Where was this, Ceil?" Richard wanted to know.

"In Miami. Back when I was working as an assistant producer for that morning TV show. We had six or seven of the contestants for the Miss Universe pageant come on the show: Miss U.S.A., Miss Spain, Miss Argentina. Of course, they were all very beautiful. But one girl stood out."

"You mean she was absolutely more beautiful than all the rest?" Frank asked.

"Not physically she wasn't. You might not have said that. She *was* gorgeous, but her beauty radiated from something inside of her. I remember only some of her physical traits—that she had long black hair and clear, alert, intelligent eyes. What I remember most, however, was that I was supposed to interview these girls and ask them, 'What do you do?' You know, did they go to school, were they scuba diving instructors, or ballerinas, or what. And this girl—I only remember she was from a South American country—was the only one that asked *me* a question. She wanted to know more about my job—what *I* was about.

"And I thought to myself, 'Now that's a caring person. Someone who is not just absorbed in herself and in her own life.'"

"So who won the Miss Universe contest that year?" Richard inquired. "Was your 'caring person' anywhere in the running?"

"Yes, indeed!" I said. "She actually won the whole thing."

"Caring matters, huh?" Richard said.

"Evidently," I said, giving his arm a hug.

I looked up into the sky and tried to read the messages floating above on the outlines of the powdery white clouds. The messages I was getting seemed to be: "Relax." "Slow down." "Look at what's around you—especially people." "Give up your worry, your anxiety, and your stress."

Do you know what? I'm not really inclined to be that way at all. I'm a high-energy, hard-charging, take-on-the-world kind of woman. I'm a very fast walker and a very fast talker. I do everything *fast!* I'll even finish your sentences for you—if you let me. About twenty years ago, however, I was in an automobile crash where I fractured my pelvis. And I had trouble walking for a long time after that. I had to walk with a walker.

What I remember is that people were always pushing past me, almost pushing me aside, because I was slowing them down on the sidewalk. I felt very vulnerable.

Now, when I may tend to get impatient about somebody taking a long time to finish something, I catch myself and remember when I, too, had to take it very slowly. For instance, recently I watched a woman sew a button on a shirt I had brought her to fix. She did it very slowly. My normal reaction would be to say to her, "Come on, *pul-leeze*…. Can't you get that done a little faster?" But I stopped myself and didn't say anything. Instead, I thought, "Mmmm. That woman must have a lot of *sensitivity* to be so careful in how she sews on that button."

I think we create a lot of our emotional distress by expecting everybody to think and act just like we do. People are *different*, after all. Different strengths—and different weaknesses. What a dull world this would be if everybody had exactly the same thought patterns and ways of acting!

"Mommie! You promised!" It was Elizabeth, tugging on my sleeve.

What was my daughter talking about? I realized that she must have been asking me something while I was off on a cloud thinking about the time when I had to move about with a walker. I must have muttered "no" to something she was asking for.

"The *zoo*, Mom, the *zoo*," my son, Frank, joined in. "You said that after the picnic we could all go to the *zoo!*"

"We'd better get moving then," said Richard, "because your mother and I are supposed to meet Allen and Suzanne this evening. We're going to a concert. Nickie is going to be picking you up here and bringing you back home. Remember?"

"That's cool, Dad," said Frank. "As long as we get to go to the zoo."

Just then my cell phone rang. Often, I don't even take it with me on weekends, because I like to leave my work at the office. But just in case Nickie needed to reach us, this time I did.

"Hey, Celia! Are you up for a wedding?" It was Laura, calling from Virginia this time.

"So you've moved, huh?"

"Indeed I have. And it's wonderful to be back close to family and so many friends. You were right about this."

"So what's it going to be—Arlington or Philadelphia?"

"In between somewhere, it looks like. Peter's company has decided to use some of his time in each office. But they're going to be generous about counting work time on the train as he commutes, so one thing I know for sure: we're going to be near an Amtrak station!"

"Laura, you sound so happy. When's the wedding?"

"In six weeks. Just block out the second Saturday in October, if you can, and we'll get you put up with Peter's family if you and Richard like."

"It'll just be me. Richard's got to be overseas in that period, and if I won't be intruding, I'll accept being put up. Otherwise, it's no problem for me to find a motel room."

"Ceil, I can't wait to see you. And thanks to your wise counsel, this decision became fairly easy for me. Peter liked your reasoning, too. You'll like him a lot, I know."

When I signed off with Laura I thought to myself: what a difference location makes! If you're not in the right place—or at least a place where you can feel "at home"—you are likely to suffer emotional upsetness. In Laura's case, as beautiful as the San Francisco Bay area can be from one season to the next, she was not happy there. It took coming back to the East Coast to give her that "at home" feeling again. So pay attention to your feelings in regard to where you live and where you work. Being in the right place is one of the essential elements in avoiding emotional distress.

-»- -»- -»- -»- ⸙ -«- -«- -«- -«-

At the Pittsburgh zoo we strolled through acres of gorgeous fauna and rock outcroppings viewing elephants, zebras, giraffes, and tigers in habitats resembling their native lands. We watched monkeys cavort and seals and sea lions splash around luscious blue pools of water. Richard and I were enjoying it all as much as our children were. Of course we also had the additional pleasure of watching them become enchanted by the wandering peacocks or wide-eyed over the cobras behind glass.

"Do you know something, Richard," I said. "Being here at the zoo reminds me of something I didn't want to leave out of my book."

"What ... *play?*" said Richard.

"Exactly," I responded. "Play. This is so much fun, isn't it, you all? Taking in the zoo! It's wonderful. I feel like a preteen again myself. But do you know what happens to us as adults? Typically, we forget how to play. And that is something we should *never* abandon. I think I lost my sense of play at about age twenty-five. It's taken me a long time to recapture it."

While Frank and Elizabeth went off to inspect a peacock closer up, the two of us came to the resolution that we would both do fun things at least three times a week. And to tell the truth, even that may not be enough. If we all wanted to be *really* healthy as adults, we would find time to play once every day. Play is another essential for promoting our own emotional well-being. Without it, we are all too likely to crumble into a heap of neuroses—or worse.

Later, after an early supper together at a quaint little Greek restaurant, our family of four split up for the evening. Nickie met us at the appointed spot and spirited Frank and Elizabeth off toward home for an evening of video games and a rented movie. And Richard and I headed for an outdoor concert of South American jazz. Allen and Suzanne stood waiting for us at the gate.

"Welcome to my world," Allen greeted us.

"Your world?" I asked, puzzled.

"The jazz buff, always the jazz buff," Suzanne explained.

"Ah, that's right," Richard remembered. "You used to play trumpet in a little combo, didn't you? And collected all those memorable LPs."

"Armstrong, Coltrane, Gillespie, Krupa, all the way through the alphabet to Dinah Washington or any point in between," Allen smiled.

"*Now* I remember," I said. "*That* is precisely why I thought this was such a good idea to come here…because we're putting ourselves in the hands of an expert—a jazz aficionado. I mean, what do I know about *jazz?* I like it, but I wouldn't necessarily know what would be a superb concert and what would be just so-so."

"Tonight will be superb," said Allen. "I promise you."

And it was. We sat on the lawn chairs we'd brought along, in a perfumed garden atmosphere—the wisteria, honeysuckle, and lilacs scenting the night air with something so delicious you could taste it on your tongue—and reveled in set after set of thrilling jazz pouring from a group I'd never heard of but which Allen knew and swore by. They were a blend of Andes highland pipes, dulcimer, guitars, and soft percussions. An amazing group with a sound I felt I would be carrying in my head for at least a week.

"Well, Ceil, what think you?" Suzanne asked as the intermission began and concertgoers shuffled out of their seats toward the lemonade and punch stand.

"Almost like heaven," I said, honestly. "I mean, look at us, under the stars, on this perfect late summer's evening…with the sounds and the scents in this spectacular garden. Just dreamy."

Perfect moments are free in life. You just have to be looking for them.

Richard was enjoying himself, too, and could only nod in agreement. "Find the experts," he said, "then trust them. They won't lead you astray."

And you, my readers, as you wind down your waltz through this little book, put that counsel into your heads and don't let it slip away. Much frustration is in store for whoever tries to be his or her own expert on everything. What a silly notion—that one person would be able to know it all! Instead, rely on those who truly know this or that domain—whether it be gardening, decorating, computer systems, marketing, or whatever. And in rubbing shoulders with those experts, you will indeed learn something of their skills or trades, even as you allow them to steer you in the right direction.

Toward the end of the program's second part, the South American jazz group breathed into the air a lullaby so sweet it was like a prayer.

"You practically want to get off your chair and kneel on the ground and sing 'Allelulia,'" I whispered to Suzanne.

"Amen, sister," she said.

My heart was filled with gratitude for the day, the picnic, the zoo, the Greek supper, and this marvelous concert in the company of good friends. And this overflowing feeling of thankfulness brings me to the very last suggestion I have for you as you go about "organizing the good life": Seek out a place to express your thankfulness on a regular basis. Connect with God, or your Higher Power. Find a church or synagogue or mosque close to your home and go there when they have services—whenever that may be, Friday or Saturday evening, or Sunday morning. Go and give thanks. Even if you may not agree 100 percent with the message or sermon that's being preached. And if one church doesn't suit you, move on and find one that does. Don't rest until you settle on a place that feels right for you.

The lack of genuine spirituality is one of the major reasons for the emptiness some of us experience in society today. You may have all the rest of it "together," but it is putting the spiritual piece in place that will teach you how to cope with the disappointments in your life. And also how to look forward with hope to the better things that await you, just around the next corner.

If you've been paying attention, honey, here is what I hope you got:

- Life is a banquet—there are *lots* of good things to sample. Decide now that you are not going to be a "poor soul" who is starving because you fail to see the delights that are all around you.

- True beauty radiates from the inside of you. This beauty will *always* reflect a caring spirit. Be the kind of person who is not self-absorbed, someone who notices other people and takes a genuine interest in others.

- If you look up at the clouds occasionally, try to read what they are telling you. The messages are: "Relax," "Slow down," "Give up your anxieties and your stress." Ask your Higher Power to slow you down, quiet your mind, steady your hurried pace, and break the tensions with which we all live.

- We create much of our emotional distress by expecting other people to think and act the way we do. People are *different*. Learn to appreciate those differences.

- Location makes a huge difference in the way we feel about ourselves. Listen to what your feelings are telling you about where you live and where you work. If you are "out of synch" with either, see what changes you can reasonably make to create a better atmosphere for yourself.

- Play more—or get back to playing if you've been almost totally away from it. When we "grow up," typically we forget how to play. If you want to be a happy adult, this "sense of play" is something you need to recapture.

- Don't try to be an expert on everything! It's a hopeless ambition. Rather, look for the real experts in whatever domain you want to explore—everything from cooking to getting in shape to charting a career—and lean on their expertise. The genuine experts in any field *will not lead you astray*. Trust them.

- Be grateful for what you have in life. For your own self, your mind, your spirit, your body, your talents, for the work you have, and the opportunities to enjoy such things as family, nature, friends, pets, music, art, and on and on.

- Find a place where you can express this gratitude on a regular basis—a church or synagogue or other place of worship. It is the spiritual dimension of our lives that can teach us how to handle disappointments, and how to live in hope and in joy.

-»- -»- -»- -»- ✿ -«- -«- -«- -«-

Yes, there is a nirvana; it is in leading your sheep to a
green pasture, and in putting your child to sleep,
and in writing the last line of your poem.
- *Kahlil Gibran, 1883-1931*

-»- -»- -»- -»- ✿ -«- -«- -«- -«-

Getting Started:
10 Things I'd Like to Change in My Life:

1. _____

2. _____

3. _____

4. _____

5. _____

6. _____

7. _____

8. _____

9. _____

10. _____

Reconnecting to the Good Life:
10 Things I Need to Make More Time For:

1. _____

2. _____

3. _____

4. _____

5. _____

6. _____

7. _____

8. _____

9. _____

10. _____

"Delegation is key to being an effective CEO of your life."
Errands I Can Delegate to Others:

"Showing up is 95 percent of everything."
Ways I Can "Show Up" More Often in My Life:

"Organization, my dear, can do more for your life than you would ever imagine!"
10 Things I Need to Organize:

1. _____

2. _____

3. _____

4. _____

5. _____

6. _____

7. _____

8. _____

9. _____

10. _____

"The good life means, among other things,
being as debt free as possible."
Things I Want to Pay Off:

Name of debt: Amount owed:

_____

_____

_____

_____

_____

"Be highly ethical, even when no one is watching."
Words I Live By - My Moral Code:

_____

_____

_____

_____

"People who have wonderful friends have a great life."
People With Whom I Can Create or Deepen a Friendship:

Notes:

Notes:

Resource Guide for *Organizing the Good Life*

A Return to Love (audio also available and highly recommended)
>Marianne Williamson. HarperCollins Publishers, Inc., 1992

The Aladdin Factor
>Jack Canfield, Mark Victor Hansen. Berkley Publishing Group, 1995.

All I Really Need to Know I Learned in Kindergarten
>Robert Fulghum. Ballantine Books, 1986.

Awakening Corporate Soul
>Eric Klein, John B. Izzo. FairWinds Press, 1998.

Be Heard Now (audiotape)
>Lee Glickstein. Sounds True, 1998.

Beachcombing at Miramar
>Richard Bode. Warner Books, Inc., 1997.

Building Moral Intelligence: The Seven Essential Virtues that Teach Kids to Do the Right Thing
>Michele Borba. Jossey-Bass Inc., 2001.

Business Etiquette for Dummies
>Sue Fox. Hungry Minds, Inc., 2001.

Chicken Soup for the Parent's Soul
>Raymond Aaron, Mark Victor Hansen, Kim Kirberger, Jack Canfield. Health Communications, 2000.

Do One Thing Different
>   Bill O'Hanlon. Morrow, William & Co., 1999.

Don't Sweat the Small Stuff...And It's All Small Stuff
>   Richard Carlson. Hyperion, 1997.

Drive Your People Wild Without Driving Them Crazy
>   Jennifer White. Capstone Publishing Ltd., 2001.

The E-Myth Revisited
>   Michael Gerber. HarperCollins Publishers, Inc., 1995.

Emotional Intelligence at Work
>   Hendrie Davis Weisinger, Ph.D. Jossey-Bass Inc., 1997.

Keep It Simple
>   Hazelden Meditations. Hazelden Foundation, 1989.

Life's Little Instruction Book
>   H. Jackson Brown. Rutledge Hill Press, 1991.

The Manager's Pocket Guide to Creativity
>   Alex Hiam. Human Resource Development Press, 1999.

Parents Do Make a Difference
>   Michele Borba. Jossey-Bass Inc., 1999.

Personal Finance for Dummies, 3rd Edition
>   Eric Tyson. Hungry Minds, Inc., 2000.

The Prophet
>Kahlil Gibran. Alfred A. Knopf, 1976.

The Purpose of Your Life
>Carol Adrienne. Morrow, William & Co., 1999.

Work Less, Make More
>Jennifer White. John Wiley & Sons, Inc., 1998.

Simplify Your Life: 100 Ways to Slow Down and Enjoy the Things That Really Matter
>Elaine St. James. Hyperion, 1994.

30 Days to a Simpler Life
>Connie Cox, Cris Evatt. Dutton/Plume, 1998.

1,001 Ways to Be Romantic
>Gregory Godek. Casablanca Press, 2000.

1,001 Ways to Market Your Book
>John Kremer. Open Horizon Publishing Company, 1998.

About the Author

CELIA ROCKS is president of Rocks-DeHart Public Relations, a publicity firm that specializes in promoting books, speakers, and consultants. She is a self-proclaimed escapee from rush-about living, mindless materialism, and deadening debt. Lessons learned from a number of best-selling "personal improvement" author-clients have been key to reforming her lifestyle. So has the influence of her husband, Richard, a genius at reducing things to the essentials. Celia and Richard live in joyful simplicity in Pittsburgh, Pennsylvania, with their two children, Frank and Elizabeth.

-» -» -» -» ↓ «- «- «- «-

You can find Celia at www.CeliaRocks.com. For information on *Organizing the Good Life* speaking and seminars, call her at 412-820-3004.

Please send your comments, personal stories and tips to Celia Rocks, Riverview Office Building, 811 Boyd Avenue, Suite 101, Pittsburgh, PA 15238 or to her e-mail address, CeliaRocks@aol.com.

All material published, whether on her website or in print, will be credited.